INSURGENCY

INSURGENCY

ANDREW M. SCOTT

with

DONALD P. CLARK, MAJOR, U.S.A.

R. BRUCE EHRNMAN

JOHN W. SALMON, JR.

HAROLD B. SHILL

FRANK W. TRAPNELL, CAPTAIN, U.S.A.

THE UNIVERSITY OF
NORTH CAROLINA PRESS
CHAPEL HILL

Copyright © 1970 by
The University of North Carolina Press
All rights reserved
ISBN 978-0-8078-9774-4 (pbk.)
Library of Congress Catalog Card Number 79-123103

PREFACE

The senior author's interest in undertaking this study was stimulated by the imbalance between the importance and complexity of insurgency and the inadequacy of the literature dealing with it. Testifying before the Senate Foreign Relations Committee in May, 1966, Secretary of Defense McNamara said, "In the last eight years alone there have been no less than 164 internationally significant outbreaks of violence . . . and the trend of such conflicts is growing rather than diminishing. At the beginning of 1958 there were 23 prolonged insurgencies going on about the world. As of February 1, 1966, there were 40. Further, the total number of outbreaks of violence has increased each year: in 1958, there were 34; in 1965, there were 58."

Insurgency is a difficult phenomenon to understand for it involves a variety of political, sociological, psychological, economic, and military factors as well as complex interactions among participants. Perhaps it is common for those working in a newly emerging field of inquiry to want to be too certain too soon about too many things. Certainly the literature on insurgency is interlaced with dogmatic statements on matters that do not permit dogmatism. For example, there is a seemingly ineradicable tendency for writers to try to describe the evolution of insurgent movements in terms of simplified stages of development that do not allow for the adaptability of the movements or the impact of external events.

The writings of Mao Tse-tung are interesting and stimulating and deserve to be called classics on insurgency, but they too have serious shortcomings. His pages will help the reader understand events in China in the three decades before 1949, but they cannot serve as a prescription for all insurgent movements. Mao Tse-tung was writing to justify and indoctrinate rather than to reach toward a general theory of insurgency. In any case, the basis on which he drew his conclusions—his own experience—was too narrow to allow for the erection of a highly general theory. For example, he emphasized the importance to the insurgents of having a vast territory in which to operate; yet, an insurgency was able to maintain itself for years on the tiny island of Cyprus. He offered a three-stage theory of insurgent development, climaxing in the stage of conventional war, yet Castro's insurgency in Cuba achieved victory without ever entering the third stage.

The literature on insurgency is unanalytic, and few studies go beyond simple formulations and the enumeration of factors deemed to be important to an insurgent movement. Analytic rigor, of the kind that could be provided by individuals able to use the tools and insights of the academic disciplines, has been conspicuously lacking.

During the academic year 1967–68 the senior author and a number of graduate students in his seminar in international politics at the University of North Carolina undertook an intensive study of insurgent movements. An approach to the subject, different from that found in other writings on the subject of insurgency, was soon developed. Tools of economic analysis were pressed into use from time to time. Economic analysis is designed to handle problems of the kind that characterize insurgency: scarcity of resources; the need to economize on resources; the desirability of finding the most efficient and economic combinations of resources; the conversion of inputs into outputs; the substitutability of resources. In addition, the approach has been shaped by the perspectives of systems analysis. An insurgent movement is viewed as a system of inputs and outputs directed by control elements. The same view is taken of counterinsurgency. Conflict between the two is also viewed in terms of systems analysis. The volume deals only with insurgency and counterinsurgency, but some of the perspectives it offers and the tools it puts to use can perhaps be applied to conventional warfare as well.

There are seven chapters in this book. The introductory chapter defines insurgency, examines some of its evolutionary aspects, and notes the difference between regular warfare and irregular warfare. Chapter II analyzes the three main types of insurgency (civil insurgency, insurgency against an invading army, insurgency against a colonial power). Chapter III offers a dynamic model of the working of an insurgent movement and the interaction between insurgent and counterinsurgent.

Chapter IV discusses the basic input factors in an insurgency and explores the way in which these factors may be substituted one for another. Chapter V treats the context of insurgency. Chapter VI examines the strategy and tactics of insurgency, and Chapter VII offers a parallel treatment of counterinsurgency. Lessons for both the insurgents and the counterinsurgents can be found in the volume, but the authors have been primarily concerned with analysis rather than with prescription or norms. It does not assume that counterinsurgency is good and insurgency is bad or the reverse.

The authors are indebted to the Department of Political Science at The University of North Carolina at Chapel Hill for a grant supporting this research. Three members of the original team working on this project had to drop out because of other responsibilities. They were Mrs. William Chandler, Nyle Frank, and Gernot Koehler, and the authors wish to acknowledge their important contributions to the study. The senior author is grateful to the University Research Council of The University of North Carolina at Chapel Hill for its support of this project.

ANDREW M. SCOTT
DONALD P. CLARK, MAJOR, U.S.A.
R. BRUCE EHRNMAN
JOHN W. SALMON, JR.
HAROLD B. SHILL
FRANK W. TRAPNELL, CAPTAIN, U.S.A.

Chapel Hill, January 1969

CONTENTS

PREFACE v

I. INTRODUCTION 3

II. A TYPOLOGY OF INSURGENCY 14

III. INSURGENCY AND COUNTERINSURGENCY: A MODEL 28

IV. INPUTS, OUTPUTS, AND SUBSTITUTABILITY 51

V. THE CONTEXT OF INSURGENCY 72

VI. INSURGENT STRATEGY AND TACTICS 89

VII. THE COUNTERINSURGENT 113

SELECTED BIBLIOGRAPHY 133

INDEX 137

INSURGENCY

CHAPTER I
INTRODUCTION

INSURGENCY DEFINED

▬▬▬ Insurgency, an intriguing blend of the old and the new, has probably enjoyed more frequent use during the last two and a half decades than at any other time in history. In the sixth century B.C., the Chinese tactician and military historian Sun Tzu engaged in insurgency and also analyzed it perceptively. Insurgencies occurred during the Peloponnesian Wars, 431–404 B.C. Later, insurgent tactics were used by the Romans against Hannibal and by the Gauls against Caesar. The Old Testament describes the use of insurgent methods by the Maccabees against the armies of Syria. Rogers's Rangers used insurgent techniques during the French and Indian War. Francis Marion, the "Swamp Fox," was active in the Carolinas in the Revolutionary War. The term *guerrilla*, or little war, was coined to refer to the insurgent resistance of the Spanish against the invading French armies during the years 1807 to 1814. Russian insurgents harassed Napoleon's retreating army in Russia in 1812, and from 1821 to 1827 Greek insurgents operated against the Ottoman Empire. In 1847, during the Mexican City campaign, General Scott was hampered by insurgents. Hungarian insurgents harassed the troops of the Austro-Hungarian Empire during 1848 and 1849. During the American Civil War, General Mosby utilized insurgent tactics in the Shenandoah Valley. In 1898, the Boers used insurgent tactics against the British in South Africa.

During the First World War, T. E. Lawrence and the Arabs fought the Turks in the Middle East. Mao Tse-tung engaged in insurgent activities in China intermittently from 1926 until his final victory over Chiang Kai Shek and the Kuomintang. During World War II, Tito and Mikhailovitch conducted insurgent operations against the German armies in Yugoslavia, the French "Maquis" acted against the German occupying forces, and Russian insurgents harassed German forces inside the

Soviet Union. Since the end of World War II there have been many insurgencies, including the Huks in the Philippines, Ho Chi Minh in Indo China, Castro in Cuba, and the Algerian and Malayan insurgencies.

These examples indicate that insurgency has a lengthy history and that it has seemed to gain prominence during the recent era. The explanation for this development appears to lie in the conjunction of several factors, no one of which would be adequate by itself. First, there is the almost Protean capacity of insurgent forces to adapt militarily to changes in the techniques and capabilities of regular armed forces. This explains how insurgent movements can survive, but it does not, of course, explain the popularity of insurgency. The explanation for its popularity may lie in the characteristics of the international environment in this era and the way in which insurgency meets the needs of various actors in that environment.

During the years of bitter Cold War antagonism, the great powers contented with one another directly and indirectly, in many places and in many ways, and insurgency played a part in this contention.[1]

Contention among the great powers (or those associated with the great powers) by means of insurgency has seemed to be a relatively safe and tolerable form of conflict in the era of thermonuclear warheads and intercontinental missiles. It is a form of limited warfare that appears controllable.

The capacity of nations to induce, direct, and support insurgencies in other nations has increased markedly in this century. This is an important aspect of the general increase in the capacity of one nation to influence the internal processes of another nation.[2]

Many new nations have emerged on the world scene, and they face a complex array of little-understood problems. Groups within these nations are sometimes eager to oppose and overthrow established governments.[3]

---

1. The Greek Civil War is an example of indirect great power competition. The involvement of communist great powers has been indirect in the Vietnam War. Such insurgencies as the First Indochina War and the Malayan insurrection can be viewed as East-West Confrontations, though they involved no great powers directly.

2. See Andrew M. Scott, *The Revolution in Statecraft: Informal Penetration* (New York: Random House, 1965).

3. "The relative immunity to insurgency of highly complex industrial societies, at one extreme, and of homogeneously integrated traditional communities, at the other, points to the crucial reason why the problem

Armed civilians have ceased to be a match for trained and determined military forces in direct confrontation. This means that, other things being equal, the street riot and the spontaneous insurrection in a city are not likely to be effective. If the armed forces of a government are to be defeated, they must be fought according to the ways of the insurgent.

Insurgency has appeared as an attractive mode of conflict because it confers certain advantages upon the insurgents, creates problems for the government, and is a relatively economic way of contesting with a government. Under some circumstances it may be the only feasible way to engage the government militarily.

It provides the insurgents with a way to challenge a government politically at the same time that it challenges it militarily. Physical resistance is more effective if it is associated with a political program and political-psychological agitation. In this way it can liberate energies that would otherwise be unavailable.

The term *insurgency* in this volume refers to efforts to obtain political goals by an organized and primarily indigenous group (or groups) using protracted, irregular warfare and allied political techniques. This definition excludes sudden coups, short-lived outbreaks of violence, or invasion by nonindigenous guerrilla forces.[4]

This definition describes pure insurgency, but obviously there is room for considerable variation in the elements that comprise the definition. For example, no fine line can be drawn in determining when a conflict is protracted and when it is not. Likewise there appears to be no a priori way of specifying how great a degree of outside intervention would be compatible with a movement's remaining primarily indigenous.

---

of insurgency is so closely related at this time in history to the transitional and underdeveloped new nations of the world. The process of social and psychological disruption that accompanies the downfall of traditional societies opens the way to a host of sharp cleavages within such societies. A general sense of social insecurity may intensify the urge to seek the sense of identity that comes from loyalty to ethnic, regional, or other traditional and parochial associations. At the same time, the process of cultural diffusion, which strikes a society at an uneven rate, can create new divisions between those who are more modernized and those who cling to the old." Lucian W. Pye in Harry Eckstein, ed., *Internal War: Problems and Approaches* (New York: Free Press, 1964), pp. 163–64.

4. This is a more restricted concept than that of "internal war" which has come into use during recent years. See Harry Eckstein, ed., *Internal War: Problems and Approaches* (New York: Free Press, 1964).

INSURGENCY AS AN EVOLUTIONARY PHENOMENON

Insurgency is ancient, but it is not timeless in the sense that it is unchanging. On the contrary, insurgency is evolutionary and developmental. There appear to have been three major pressures causing its evolution. First, the desire of individual insurgents to survive and the desire of leaders to keep their movements in existence has led to adaptation. For example, when regular forces began to use aircraft for spotting and attack, insurgents responded variously by operating in smaller units, moving at night, breaking camp frequently, using natural cover, storing materials underground, and sometimes living underground. When counterinsurgent forces began to use trucks and armored cars in their operations, insurgents responded by leaving the roads and moving into areas in which road-bound forces could not operate.

A second pressure for insurgent adaptation has lain in the continuing desire of insurgents to take advantage of the vulnerabilities of regular forces to strike at those forces more effectively. The operations of regular forces have evolved with time and with the circumstances of various conflicts, and this in turn has induced a corresponding evolution in the techniques of insurgency. Generally speaking, the military practices of the insurgents evolve in response to changes in the technology and activities of regular forces. Radio began to be used by counterinsurgents and was soon pressed into use by insurgents for their own purposes. The counterinsurgents in Vietnam increased their fire power to deal with the insurgents, and the latter responded by making use of light mortars and rockets. As regular forces began to use armored vehicles and truck-born troops, the insurgents responded with increased use of the land mine and the ambush.

While the pressure for adaptation is normally greater for the insurgent than the counterinsurgent because of the unequal nature of the military forces involved, the behavior of the counterinsurgent is also likely to be adaptive to at least some extent. The following pattern might be fairly typical. The government forces may begin the cycle by altering their tactics or utilizing a new weapon or device. This changed behavior represents a challenge to the insurgent forces. They respond to the challenge by taking actions designed to reduce their vulnerability to the new behavior of the government. For example, if the innovation is increased use of modern transport, the insurgent's response may be to avoid those surroundings in which such transport offers a significant advantage. The insurgent may also respond to the challenge by striking at the transportation system, destroying railroad tracks, engines, switching yards, airfields, roads, bridges, tunnels.

This response on the part of the insurgent will probably be perceived by the counterinsurgents as a new challenge. They will respond by trying to minimize the response options available to the insurgent. If the insurgent has responded to the use of aircraft by relying upon dispersion, concealment, and night movement, the counterinsurgent might respond by developing night scopes, infrared photography, and defoliation. Such a development will represent a new challenge to the insurgent, and another round of the challenge-response cycle will be under way.

The third major pressure for insurgent adaptation derives from the continuing desire of insurgent leaders to take advantage of the opportunities that the environment as a whole offers them. In a period in which ideologies may be powerful movers of men, insurgent leaders have sometimes become influential ideologues. Because political organization and agitation are often effective weapons in the twentieth century, insurgent leaders now give these elements prominence. As the springs of loyalty have become better understood, the psychological warfare aspects of insurgent operations have become more important. The increasing capacity of nations or groups to reach inside other nations and influence their activities has been reflected in changes in the behavior of insurgents. Insurgent leaders have learned that they can sometimes find foreign support and backing for their movements. In recent decades, many civil insurgencies have been internationalized by the intervention of foreign powers.

INSURGENCY: STAGES OF DEVELOPMENT

Analysts and activists alike have been attracted by the idea of developing a theory of insurgent development. This has typically taken the form of presenting a series of stages through which all insurgents' movements were thought to have to pass. The best known formulation of this kind is Mao Tse-tung's three-stage theory of development: (1) protracted conflict, (2) mobile conflict, (3) conventional warfare. As these theories have been presented they share a common defect. Insurgent movements are treated as if their developmental patterns were predetermined. Each movement is expected to move forward from stage to stage with no detours, no false starts, no failures, and no skipping of stages.

It is possible to use the concept of stages in a much more flexible and illuminating way. The normal range of political and legal activity can be distinguished from insurgency, and both can be distinguished from conventional warfare. Three easily identifiable phases that a movement might enter are the legal-political, insurgent, and conventional war phases.

A political organization operating in the legal-political phase might be unable to acquire office legally and might turn to insurgency, moving from phase A to phase B. This is represented by case 1 in figure 1. The insurgency might continue for a time and then abate (case 2), or it might revert to being a legal-political movement once again (case 3). It might move into a conventional war phase (case 4). This, of course, was Mao Tse-tung's experience in the Chinese Civil War. The evolution of a movement is not foreordained however.

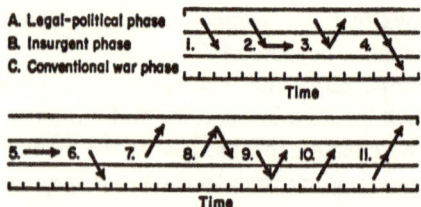

A. Legal-political phase
B. Insurgent phase
C. Conventional war phase

Fig. 1.

A movement might never go through a legal-political phase but begin as an insurgency. It might continue as an insurgency (case 5), move into a conventional war phase (case 6), or move into a legal-political phase (case 7). It could, of course, move into the other phases and then back to insurgency (cases 8 and 9). General Vo Nguyen Giap, for example, eschewed conventional warfare against the French after the disastrous Red River campaign of 1950. The Vietminh, it should be noted, began in the legal-political phase.

It is possible for a conventional war to move into an insurgent phase after the regular forces have been defeated (case 10). Although unlikely, such a movement might ultimately pass into a legal-political phase (case 11). Other variations are possible, but the point has already been made. Insurgent movements do not all begin at the same place, do not follow the same paths of development, and do not develop at the same rate. Because these figures relate time (on the horizontal axis) and intensity of conflict (on the vertical axis), it is possible to use these axes to depict the life history of a movement. For example it is possible to trace the development of a movement as it moves up the intensity scale while in the legal-political phase. Activities associated with normal electoral politics might be replaced, in ascending order of intensity, by demonstrations, politically motivated strikes, politically motivated boycotts, civil disobedience, and rioting. The development of the movement can be traced as it moves across the threshold into insurgency. The faster the tempo of escalation (or de-escalation), the greater will be the amount of vertical movement relative to horizontal movement. In figure 2 the leaders of the movement depicted in case 12 hesitated before crossing the threshold from legal action into illegal action. Once in that second phase, however, escalation was rapid, and conventional warfare soon commenced.

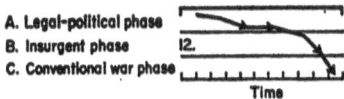

Fig. 2.

A movement need not operate at a single level of intensity, of course. At any given moment its activities may cover a sizable portion of the intensity spectrum. It is possible, for example, for a movement conducting conventional war to engage in insurgent activities at the same time.

The rate at which a movement develops will depend on a

variety of factors, including the purposes of the leaders, their competence, the amount of opposition that the movement encounters, and its capacity to overcome various growth crises. One such crisis may come when the movement is forced to maintain its organization around the clock and no longer dissolves during the daytime. Another crisis may come when it first attracts serious opposition from the counterinsurgents and begins to suffer significant losses.

INSURGENCY AND IRREGULAR WARFARE

Insurgency and irregular warfare are not the same thing. The term irregular warfare refers only to military activities. Insurgency, on the other hand, has both military and political components. Insurgency is irregular warfare plus politics. Irregular warfare is insurgency minus politics.

Irregular warfare must be defined in terms of its difference from regular warfare. The changing characteristics of regular warfare suggest that the characteristics of irregular warfare must also change, and an examination of irregular warfare in different historical periods confirms this. Because of the evolution of irregular warfare, a search for its essence is not very fruitful. There appears to be no single feature of combat that, in all times and places, clearly distinguishes regular warfare from irregular warfare. The term irregular warfare is a useful one, but the phenomenon that the term signifies is characterized by a cluster of related features rather than by a single feature.

Insurgency has already been defined. In the pages that follow, an effort will be made to describe it at greater length. If the section on the political-psychological dimension of insurgency were set aside, the description remaining would be that of irregular warfare.

THE POLITICAL-PSYCHOLOGICAL DIMENSION

The political-psychological aspects of insurgency are prominent and important.

The environment relevant to insurgent conflict is dominated less by terrain and physical factors and more by human beings and psychological factors than is the environment for regular warfare.

Victory and defeat are measured less in terms of tangibles (enemy soldiers killed, units destroyed, square miles of ground occupied) than intangibles such as shifts in popular support, altered perceptions, and altered behavior on the part of segments of the populace.

Military successes (or defeats) will often have profound political and psychological consequences. Therefore military activities are planned with an eye to their potential political-psychological impact. If either side fails to give adequate weight to the political-psychological impact of its activities, it will be placed at a severe disadvantage.

The civil population plays a more important role in insurgent conflict than in regular warfare as it has been waged through most of history. Instead of being distant from the battlefield, the civil population is the battlefield. Combatants are not restricted to those in uniform.

LEADERSHIP AND INTELLIGENCE

Leadership is likely to be personalized, relatively charismatic, and nonbureaucratic.

The gulf between officers and enlisted men—a prominent feature of regular armies—is likely to be less prominent in irregular forces.

Fewer of the leaders will be professional military men.

Leadership will be based more on achievement than ascription.

The political and military functions of leadership will be intertwined at all levels.

The insurgent intelligence apparatus will normally be less professional than that of the counterinsurgents, will involve less of a division of labor, and is likely to be technically less sophisticated than that of the counterinsurgents, although not necessarily less effective.

ORGANIZATION, COMMUNICATIONS, RECRUITMENT

Organizational structure will be less elaborate, and there will be less division of labor.

Individual units and field commands are likely to have relatively more autonomy than corresponding units in regular armies.

Insurgent organization is likely to be characterized by many small units.

These units are likely to be more self-contained than conventional military units.

The communications system possessed by the irregular forces is likely to be less sophisticated technically than that possessed by the regular forces facing them.

Recruitment is based normally on voluntary rather than compulsory service.

EQUIPMENT AND LOGISTICS

The equipment of the insurgents will usually be less sophisticated than that of the counterinsurgents, and some items will be homemade.

Equipment will tend to be lighter than that of regular forces.

Equipment is likely to be miscellaneous rather than standardized since it may have come from a variety of sources, including the enemy.

Equipment will normally be scarce, and certain categories of it may be lacking altogether. Ammunition is frequently in short supply.

Equipment repair and shortage of storage facilities will normally create severe problems for the insurgent.

The insurgent force will have special logistical problems because of the clandestine nature of the enterprise, the risk involved in supply operations, and the easily identifiable nature of most military equipment and supplies. Commercial channels can rarely be used to any extent for freight, and the use of roads and railroads will present formidable problems.

Insurgent movements often have sources of supply outside the country.

TRAINING

Precombat training is likely to be short in duration and skimpy, by conventional standards, because of lack of time, shortage of specialized personnel, and lack of ammunition.

Insurgent training is likely to place a greater emphasis upon political indoctrination than will conventional military training.

DISCIPLINE AND MORALE

Insurgent movements typically place less emphasis on the formalities of military courtesy than do conventional forces.

Discipline depends less on formal obligations and fear of punishment and more on morale, devotion to the cause, camaraderie, and peer group reinforcement.

Insurgent movements lack the involved bureaucratic apparatus and procedures that support discipline in most conventional forces.

Insurgent enforcement of discipline is likely to be characterized by informality, flexibility, speed, and harshness.

Insurgent morale is likely to be influenced heavily by immediate success (or lack of it) and therefore may be more mercurial than that of conventional forces.

The rate of insurgent defection is likely to be closely related to the success of the movement, and that is one reason insurgent leaders frequently feel they cannot afford even temporary defeat.

Because of the relationship of defection to morale, and because of the lack of capacity to take reprisals against the defector or his family, defection is often a problem for insurgent forces.

TACTICS AND COMBAT

An insurgency will place a greater emphasis on the use of stealth, concealment, and surprise than will regular forces.

Frontal warfare and positional warfare will normally be avoided.

A heavy reliance will be placed upon hit and run tactics.

Insurgents will try to break off contact with the enemy rather than maintain it.

Great emphasis will be placed upon tactical mobility (which does not necessarily mean mechanization).

Highly favorable conditions will be sought before an engagement is allowed to develop.

The insurgent will not hesitate to avoid engaging a dangerous force.

The insurgent is likely to plan military operations with an awareness of their political and psychological implications.

Unable to beat the regular forces at their own game, the insurgents elect to play by a quite different set of rules, one that favors them. By utilizing techniques of the kind indicated above, an insurgent movement can survive, though facing a far more powerful enemy, and may even be able to induce regular units to give up the struggle.

CHAPTER II
A TYPOLOGY OF INSURGENCY

The different types of internal warfare have been classified in a variety of ways in accordance with the identity of the revolutionaries, their objectives or goals, the level of violence employed, or the targets of the movement. These criteria are not always consistent and tend to produce numerous and overlapping subcategories such as coups d'etat, militarized mass insurrection, palace revolution, national revolution, revolutionary wars, civil wars, and nonconstitutional transfers of power.[1]

This volume is concerned with a single type of internal war —insurgency. Before the analysis of insurgency can proceed, however the main types of insurgency must be distinguished. The basis for the distinction used here is the character of the counterinsurgents, and when this standard is applied, three types of insurgency emerge: civil insurgency, anticolonial insurgency, and insurgency against an invading or occupying army. Each of these types has characteristic features.

TYPES OF INSURGENCY
CIVIL INSURGENCY

If the counterinsurgents are an autonomous, indigenous government or an indigenous ruling elite, the insurgency is classified as a civil insurgency since both the insurgents and the counterinsurgents are indigenous.

---

1. Several studies have generated typologies of civil violence based on quantitative techniques. For examples see R. J. Rummel, "Dimensions of Conflict Behavior within Nations, 1946–59," *Journal of Conflict Resolution* 10 (March 1966): 65–73 and Raymond Tanter and Manus Midlarsky, "A Theory of Revolution," *Journal of Conflict Resolution* 11 (September 1967): 264–80.

ANTICOLONIAL INSURGENCY

An insurgency is termed anticolonial if the insurgents are drawn from the controlled country and if their efforts are directed against an outside or colonial power that controls the country's decision-making processes.

Sometimes only a fine line can be drawn between military administration by an occupying army and the governing of a colonial territory. Usually, however, the invading or occupying army will lack the status inside an occupied country that may be enjoyed by a colonial region. During an anticolonial insurgency, the colonial power may even be able to recruit troops from the nationals of the country that is being dominated. An invading force would normally have little success in this direction. In addition, the methods of control used by a colonial regime will be primarily political rather than military. The military forces that the colonial power maintains are there for garrison purposes and not for conducting major military operations.

INSURGENCY AGAINST AN INVADING OR OCCUPYING ARMY

The third type of insurgency is that against an invading or occupying army. Most instances falling in this category are readily identifiable. Prime examples are the efforts of the French, Russian, and Yugoslav partisans against the German forces during the Second World War.

This type of insurgency involves the conduct of irregular warfare in areas occupied by an invader. It may be conducted in conjunction with a regular army or by itself after the regular army has been defeated or withdrawn. Unlike the other two types of insurgency, it is not antigovernmental. Indeed, the government of the country invaded may be directing the insurgents or working with them while in hiding or in exile. It is internal war only in the sense that it is being fought within the country's boundaries by an irregular citizen army. In substance, the struggle is really between the forces or peoples of two separate nations.

In a colonial situation, as noted above, the colonial power exercises control largely by political means. In the case of military occupation, however, primary reliance is placed upon military means. If a territory were to be shifted from occupation status to colonial status, this change would be effected by diminishing the role of military instruments of control and increasing the role of civil instruments of control.

GENESIS OF INSURGENCY[2]

In order to understand the genesis of insurgency one must consider the setting in which it takes place, the preconditions for insurgency, and the initiating event.

PRECONDITIONS

The setting of a potential insurgency includes many situational factors. These situational factors may (or may not) satisfy the preconditions of insurgency. Four preconditions for insurgency must be satisfied to some degree before an insurgency can be initiated:

1. Hostility to the controlling political or military power
2. The existence of a discontented elite willing to provide organization and leadership
3. A relatively widespread acknowledgment of the necessity for the use of nonlegitimate or violent means to achieve political goals or to obtain redress
4. The capacity to conduct insurgent conflict

These preconditions need not invariably be satisfied in the same way. Indeed it is likely that they will be satisfied in quite different ways depending upon the type insurgency involved.

PRECONDITIONS: CIVIL INSURGENCY

Numerous situational factors may help satisfy preconditions for a civil insurgency.

  a. low level (or low sense) of political participation leading to a low level of support for the regime in power

2. For quantitative studies exploring social, economic, and political factors underlying civil violence see: Tanter and Midlarsky, "Theory of Revolution;" Ted Gurr, "Psychological Factors in Civil Violence," *World Politics* 20 (January 1968): 245–78; Ted Gurr, "A Causal Model of Civil Strife: A Comparative Analysis Using New Indices," *American Political Science Review* 67 (December 1968): 1104–24; and Ivo Feierabend and Rosalind Feierabend, "Aggressive Behavior within Politics, 1948–62: A Cross-National Study," *Journal of Conflict Resolution* 10 (September 1966): 249–71.

b. discontent with the quality of life under the present regime
c. discontent with the policies of the present regime
d. existence of isolated and alienated elites which are denied access to the instruments of legitimate political power and which can arouse latent hostility and provide leadership and organization to the discontented
e. ban on normal political opposition which might have the effect of forcing the discontented to express their dissatisfaction by illegitimate or violent action
f. inadequacy of communications channels between the regime and the masses
g. widely felt inequality in the distribution of important values in the society
h. lack of a tradition disapproving of the use of violence or of illegitimate means to achieve political goals or redress grievances
i. existence of racial, ethnic, linguistic, or class segments of the population that are excluded from the political processes of the society
j. existence of groups ready to capitalize on anti-regime sentiments and to channel discontent into action
k. emergence of an attractive ideology incompatible with the existing social or political system

Factors such as these can combine to create the preconditions for insurgency. External factors could have some influence, but in civil insurgencies internal conditions are likely to play the dominant role. While nationalism provides the momentum for colonial and antioccupation insurgencies, social, economic, and ideologic cleavages provide the drive in civil conflict.

PRECONDITIONS: ANTICOLONIAL INSURGENCY

It is difficult for a colonial nation, even an enlightened colonial nation, to avoid taking actions which will lay the groundwork for insurgency. Hostility to foreigners, which is likely to be produced under the best of circumstances, is almost certain to be increased if the foreigners occupy a dominant position in a country. Formal subordination to foreign rule helps to create the preconditions for insurgency. It unites people and provides a focus for nationalist sentiment. The charge of economic exploitation by the colonial country is likely to be effective in stirring men to action. The doctrine of national self-determination is always at hand and can provide whatever theoretical justification is needed for a nationalist movement. Those situational factors, mentioned in the previous section, that help create the preconditions for civil insurgency may also contribute to the development of insurgency against a colonial power.

In the case of anticolonial insurgency, local elites are usually quick to volunteer to lead the struggle against the colonial nation. Among these may be nationals the colonial power has educated in the mother country. To be sure, individual nationals may be co-opted by the colonial power and serve as a brake on the development of insurgent sentiment.

PRECONDITIONS: INSURGENCY AGAINST AN INVADING OR OCCUPYING ARMY

One of the preconditions for insurgency is hostility toward the controlling regime. This precondition is almost automatically satisfied in the case of a foreign invasion or military occupation. The same is true of the need for a discontented elite willing to provide organization and leadership to the insurgent movement. The third precondition, a readiness to use force, is also customarily satisfied when a nation is invaded.

The difficulty is likely to center around the fourth precondition, the capacity to conduct insurgent conflict. The factors that contribute to the capacity to resist would include the following.

a. absence of complete population control by the invader
b. will to resist
c. belief in the feasibility of resistance
d. leadership and organization
e. sources of supply

PRECIPITATING EVENT

It does not follow that if the preconditions for insurgency are satisfied insurgency will instantly erupt. The conflict must await a precipitating event. Figure 1 may be helpful in indicating the relationships among situational factors, preconditions, initiating event, and insurgency.

An initiating event takes place within the setting and is of such a nature that it serves to mobilize the energies of the discontented and to direct them toward violent action. Its

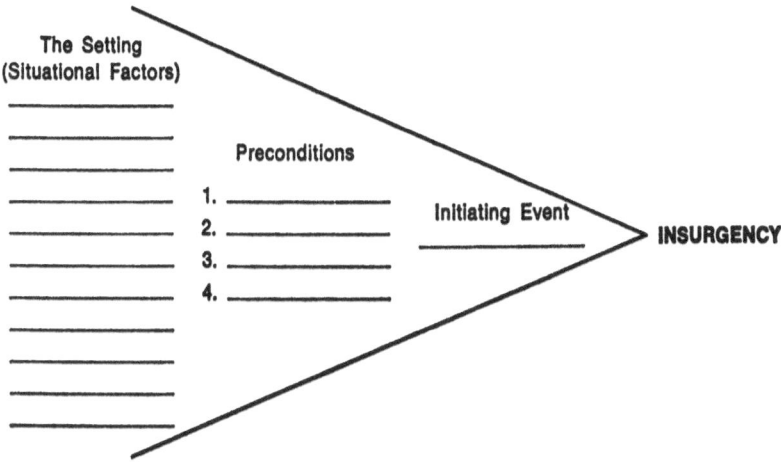

Fig. 1.

impact is psychological rather than purely physical, and the impact need not follow immediately upon the event. The event may have little intrinsic significance but may be seized upon at some point by an elite or organization and may be given a special significance. A listing of possible initiating events would include the following.

a. an event which acquires symbolic significance such as an economic or social disaster, a particularly antagonizing action by the regime, or a heroic act of defiance by an individual rebel
b. an event that forces action, such as an invasion by a foreign power
c. the emergence of a charismatic leader
d. the perception of a tactical or strategic advantage by a revolutionary elite
e. the decision by a revolutionary elite to issue a call to arms
f. the influence of foreign agents or propaganda

The more ripe the time, the greater is the range of events from which the initiating event can be drawn. If the situation is explosive (which is to say some or all of the preconditions have been satisfied to a high degree), almost any event may serve as an initiating event. The ripeness of time may also produce a flood of events in a short period of time so that it would be difficult to point to a single event as the act that precipitated the struggle. In such a situation it may be more helpful to think of a series of acts as precipitants.

OBJECTIVES OF INSURGENT MOVEMENTS

Any discussion of the objectives of insurgent movements must distinguish between formal objectives and informal, unannounced objectives. Followers may be exhorted in terms of one set of objectives, and actual planning may move forward in terms of a quite different set. Informal objectives, that are likely to deal with questions of political tactics and personal advantage, are important for the leadership even if they tend not to be suitable for exploitation and the winning of broad support.

Tito's formal objective was driving the Germans out of Yugoslavia, but his informal objectives included the acquisition of political power by the Communist party and himself once the Germans departed. This meant the Chetnik movement had to be discredited and destroyed since it was a potential competitor for power. The formal objective of the French resistance was the defeat of the Germans. Informally, however, each of the major factions sought to strengthen its political position and to weaken that of the opposition in preparation for the postwar showdown.

OBJECTIVES: CIVIL INSURGENCY

The formal objectives of an insurgency might be arranged along a continuum. At one end would be minimum objectives such as minor reforms. At the other end would be an objective such as the complete reorganization of society. Between the extremes would be objectives such as achievement of significant reforms, participation in the government, control of the government, overthrow of the government, and modification of the entire political system.

During the course of an insurgency objectives are likely to evolve. Typically the demands of the insurgents escalate as the struggle begins, as blood is spilled, as relations become embittered, and as the insurgents devote more thought to the reasons for their discontent. Later, if victory is not achieved, the insurgents may be forced to reduce their demands in order to settle the conflict. Extreme demands may be excellent for morale, but they may also prolong conflict.

OBJECTIVES: ANTICOLONIAL INSURGENCY

The major complaints of those trying to organize an anticolonial insurgency are, customarily, inadequate participation in decision-making, economic exploitation, and denial of self-determination. These complaints may be restated by the discontented in terms of positive objectives: expropriation of foreign holdings in the country, ouster of all foreign nationals, independence, and establishment of a noncolonial governing system.

OBJECTIVES: ANTIOCCUPATION INSURGENCY

The primary objective in an insurgency against an invading army is the expulsion of the enemy from the country. There may be secondary objectives such as institution of a new political regime, once the enemy has departed, or achievement of significant social reforms.

BASIC INPUT FACTORS

Input factors common to the three kinds of insurgency are examined in chapter IV. Here, however, the aim is simply to note the way in which the role of these inputs may vary depending on the type of insurgency involved.

LEADERSHIP AND ORGANIZATION

Leadership in a civil insurgency may come from an established political or economic elite or from a class whose members feel that they have been cut off from the exercise of political power. Some of the leadership in a civil insurgency may come from outside the country. Such outside assistance may be either voluntary on the part of the individuals concerned or may be part of a governmental program.

Leadership in an anticolonial insurgency may come from any of the sources mentioned above, but it is more likely to come from the educated and propertied classes in this instance than it is in the case of civil insurgency. However, leadership in an insurgency against an invading or occupying army is a somewhat different matter. The insurgency is likely to be sponsored by the legitimate government in exile. Regular army officers may play a prominent role as Red Army officers did in the Soviet Union after the German invasion in 1942. Leadership may come from the same sources as in an anticolonial insurgency or a civil insurgency, but it is more likely to be exerted by those elites that would exercise legitimate power if the country were not occupied by a foreign army. If the insurgency is being underwritten by an allied government interested in continuing the struggle against the invader, leadership will be offered by foreign officers. This was the case with the British in Norway and the Americans in the Philippines during World War II.

LOGISTIC SUPPORT

During a civil insurgency the insurgents are apt to have difficulty obtaining weapons and supplies because the various sources for this material may be inadequate.

1. Theft or seizure. Theft cannot provide a continuous flow of supplies and the volume of supplies from this source is also likely to be small. During the early stages of a movement seizure will probably be risky. Later on, of course, seizure may become a vitally important source of supply.
2. Domestic purchase. The government is usually able to cut-off or sharply reduce the flow of weapons and supplies purchased from sources within the country. Because of the government's control of roads and railroads, the insurgent usually finds it difficult to move large quantities of material internally.
3. Foreign purchase. The insurgents are likely to suffer from a shortage of funds and will therefore find it difficult to buy needed quantities of weapons and supplies from abroad. In addition, there is the problem of smuggling the supplies into the country, given the government's control of port facilities and roads, and of distributing them.
4. Provided by a friendly foreign power. A foreign power may be willing to provide weapons and supplies. This will ease the financial burden on the insurgents but the problem of smuggling the supplies into the country and distributing them will remain. In addition, there may be a political price tag associated with this support, such as the acceptance of advisors and guidance from the foreign power.

An anticolonial insurgency is likely to be faced with similar supply problems because the colonial government will be able to control the internal transportation system if it wishes to do so. There are several features of the situation that may be more favorable, however. First, if there is widespread opposition to the colonial power, the insurgents may be able to move supplies with less fear of informers than would be experienced in the case of a civil insurgency. Second, if the wealthier segments of the society are supporting the insurgency, the financial problem may be eased to some extent.

In the case of an insurgency against an invading army or an occupying force, the supply problem will be somewhat different. Weapons may be available from regular soldiers who refused to put down their arms when the army surrendered or broke up. If there is a government in exile, it may be able to provide supplies, and a friendly power would be another possible source of supply. Internal movement of supplies will remain difficult, however, if the country is under actual occupation.

MANPOWER AND POPULATION UTILIZATION

The most important factor determining manpower practices and population utilization practices in the three different types of insurgency is the prevailing distribution of attitudes in the population. This distribution, in turn, is influenced by the experiences the population has undergone. If a country has suffered a foreign invasion, the population is likely to be easily reached by the appeals of the insurgents. The predisposition to resist will be there, and the insurgent leadership need only activate latent feelings and channel the resulting action.

Insurgents can usually take advantage of predispositions produced by a colonial experience. Nevertheless, as Thomas Jefferson noted in the Declaration of Independence, ". . . all experience hath shewn, that mankind are more disposed to suffer, while evils are sufferable, than to right themselves by abolishing the forms to which they are accustomed." If colonial rule has been longstanding, apathy may be widespread. However, such rule will also have provided grounds for complaints and dissatisfaction. If the insurgent leaders can combine these concrete complaints with a strong nationalist appeal, they are likely to have a solvent capable of removing apathy and disinterest.

In the case of a civil insurgency, on the other hand, the insurgent is usually denied a clear-cut nationalist appeal. The call to drive out the invader or to resist the colonial oppressor crosses all sections of the population and therefore can elicit society-wide support. During a civil insurgency, however, a society will be split rather than unified by the appeals made to it. The disadvantaged may be set against the advantaged, the disenfranchised against the franchised, race against race, minority against majority.

INTELLIGENCE

Each of the three types of insurgent movements requires intelligence. There appear to be differences in the nature of the intelligence requirements for each type movement, the sources from which intelligence would characteristically come, and the intelligence-gathering techniques that each would use. Since limited data is available, however, generalization will not be attempted.

STRATEGY AND TACTICS

A variety of strategies and tactics are available to the antagonists in an insurgent conflict. Which of the available strategies will be selected will depend upon the type insurgency involved and the particular circumstances surrounding that insurgency. Nevertheless, certain types of strategy are likely to be associated with certain kinds of insurgency.

STRATEGY AND TACTICS: CIVIL INSURGENCY

In this type insurgency, the insurgent faces an indigenous governing structure. Unless the members of the government choose to flee the country, they have no choice but to resist. From the point of view of the counterinsurgent leaders, resistance cannot cost more than defeat, therefore they will resist to the end. Harassment of the government, in the hope that it will give up the struggle, will probably not be a winning strategy for the insurgents.

Each side may feel somewhat restricted in the coercive measures that it can use against the populace. The use of severe measures may lead to a loss of popular support and a consequent weakening of the insurgency. This matter is discussed in a later chapter.

STRATEGY AND TACTICS: ANTICOLONIAL INSURGENCY

Insurgents fighting a colonial power will seek to raise the cost to that power of retaining the colony. The cost will be measured in money, lives, loss of international good will, and loss of political support at home. At some point, the insurgents hope, the colonial power will conclude that the colony is not worth the cost of keeping it. The war of the Viet Minh against the French in Indo China was won at Dien Bien Phu—and in Paris. The French army did not lose the war in Algeria, but the French nation concluded that the benefits from keeping Algeria a part of France did not compensate for the costs of doing so.

Pursuit of military victory is a possible strategy for the insurgent. In view of the probable disparity in military strength between insurgent and counterinsurgents, however, a strategy aimed at the opponent's will to resist may be more realistic than one aimed at direct military victory.

An anticolonial insurgency may also incorporate diplomatic elements into its overall strategy. It is usually not very difficult for an insurgent movement to muster diplomatic support from nations that are anticolonial in orientation.

STRATEGY AND TACTICS: INSURGENCY AGAINST AN INVADING OR OCCUPYING ARMY

The strategic options open to insurgents in this case are somewhat restricted. If there is an indigenous army still in the field or if an allied army continues to fight, the insurgents may be able to make a significant contribution. They may be able to harass the enemy's supply lines and communications lines and, by so doing, force the enemy to divert substantial numbers of troops from combat to population control. The resistance in Yugoslavia is commonly said to have tied down thirty-five German divisions. If a conventional army no longer remained in the field to fight the invaders, however, the effectiveness of the insurgents might be problematic. If the bulk of the German troops had not been tied up fighting conventional forces, they would probably have been able to deal with the Yugoslav partisans. It is difficult to imagine the Germans being driven out of France or the Netherlands by the resistance. The troops of the invading army are probably prepared to be ruthless, and this is an advantage to them. All chance for gaining popular support was probably dashed by the invasion, and therefore they have little left to lose and will feel free to use harsh measures against the populace.

INTERNATIONALIZATION OF INSURGENCY

Each state, colony, or territory is a part of the international system. That being the case, national politics cannot exist in a vacuum. To some extent at least domestic politics are open to the gaze of foreigners and to intervention by foreigners.[3] It is rare for an insurgency to remain untouched by foreign influence.

Insurgencies involving colonial or occupying powers are internationalized by definition. That is, the struggle is not between elements that are primarily indigenous. In civil insurgencies intervention may take any number of forms—diplomatic intervention, direct participation by a foreign power (or powers) in the conflict, or covert participation.

The logic that leads to internationalization of an insurgent conflict can be seen in the following example. An insurgency develops in country X for a variety of reasons related to internal conditions. The insurgents, hard-pressed by the government forces and badly in need of supplies, approach country Y for assistance. Country Y might consider assisting the insurgents for any of a number of reasons.

a. It is opposed to the government of X, and supporting the insurgents offers an economical, low-risk means of embarrassing that government.
b. It is opposed to another country (Z) that supports the government of X, and it sees support for the insurgents as a way to embarrass Z.
c. It is inclined to support the insurgents for ideological reasons.
d. If the insurgents were to be victorious in country X and owed their victory to Y's support, the government of Y might be influential in X and would have won the friendship of the new government of X.

3. See Andrew M. Scott, *The Revolution in Statecraft* (New York: Macmillan, 1965).

Therefore the government of Y decides to offer large-scale support to the insurgent movement. This support begins to endanger the position of the government of country X. That government, therefore, turns to country Z and seeks its support. For reasons similar to those of government Y, the government of Z offers its support to X. The conflict is now thoroughly internationalized with Y supporting the insurgents and Z supporting the government. The nature and level of the support may be such that the entire nature of the insurgency is altered, and the conflict may even become one that is primarily between the intervening nations.

CONCLUSION

This chapter has presented a typology of insurgent movements, and it has sought to examine the characteristics associated with each of the three major types. It is apparent that characteristics of one type of insurgency may not be found in the other two types. Caution should therefore be exercised in drawing conclusions on the basis of an examination of one type and assuming that these conclusions will hold for the other types as well.

CHAPTER III
INSURGENCY AND COUNTERINSURGENCY: A MODEL

▄▄▄▄ This chapter offers a general model for the analysis of insurgent-counterinsurgent conflict. The over-all model consists of several elements: an operational model and a model of the control system of each of the antagonists. These elements are related to each other as shown in figure 1.

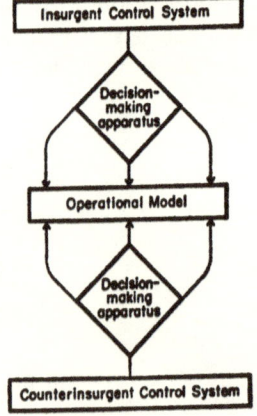

Fig. 1.

Information about the course of the conflict flows from the operational model to the control systems of both sides. The control systems process this information, in keeping with their impressions and attitudes, and generate decisions which in turn influence action in the operational model. It should be remembered throughout the subsequent discussion that the elements of the model are analytic constructs and do not necessarily possess physical analogs. To demonstrate the working of the entire model the discussion will first describe the operational model in isolation, then the control system model, and, finally, the process of conflict itself.

OPERATIONAL MODEL

Several preliminary points should be made about the operational model at the outset. First, it possesses symmetry since the key elements and the basic mechanisms that it depicts are identical for both the insurgents and the counterinsurgents. Profound differences appear at a lower level of generality, however. Both sides have capabilities, but the nature and magnitude of those capabilities will show wide variation. Both sides make judgments about strategy and tactics, but the strategic and tactical decisions will be very different.

Second, everything beyond the outer boundary of the system is a part of the international environment. The participants in the domestic struggle may be able to influence to some extent the way in which that environment impinges upon the struggle, but they will not be able to control it. Inputs from the external environment may be vague and indirect, such as a U.N. resolution eliciting a popular response within the nation. Conversely, they may be more direct, such as the provision of weapons or troops to one side or the other. The graphic model (Fig. 3) places the decision gate on such inputs outside the boundaries of the system, indicating that the crucial decisions with regard to them are made by external actors rather than by the indigenous antagonists.

Third, through the model flow physical resources and psychological responses. A flow is deemed to be physical if it has an obvious material component (weapons, supplies, men). A flow is deemed to be psychological if it is nonmaterial and has to do with morale, ideology, and the loyalties of individuals and groups. Many actions related to insurgency will, of course, produce both physical flows and psychological responses.

ARENA OF CONFLICT (A)

The discussion of the operational model can usefully begin with the arena of conflict, the hub of the model. In the arena of conflict insurgents and counterinsurgents interact, and their

30 ▪ INSURGENCY

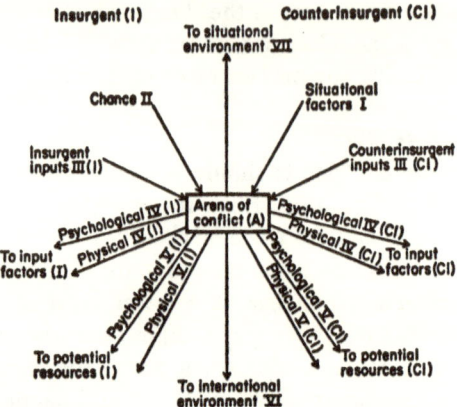

Fig. 2.

competing efforts collide. As indicated in figure 2, this arena can be thought of as a "black box" which receives the inputs of both the insurgents [III (I)] and the counterinsurgents [III (CI)]. These inputs reflect the capabilities of the antagonists and are deployed in accordance with their respective strategies and tactics (G1). In addition, there are inputs from the environment (I) and those that are products of chance (II). These inputs are processed within the box (A) and emerge as outputs (IV and V)—the results of what has taken place in the arena of conflict. These outputs may have both physical and psychological manifestations.

Figure 3 presents the full operational model. It demonstrates the dynamic features of the model and the central nature of the arena of conflict. In essence the elements added in figure 3 complete the loop between inputs to and outputs from the arena (A) and demonstrate the interconnected nature of the model within the boundaries of the system. This makes it clear that inputs into the arena (A) are processed there to produce outputs which in turn effect the nature of subsequent rounds of inputs. Thus the model depicts a dynamic, cyclic round of action in which what has gone before effects what is yet to come.

INPUTS INTO THE ARENA OF CONFLICT

More specifically, there are four types of inputs into the arena of conflict: (1) situational factors (I); (2) chance (II); (3)

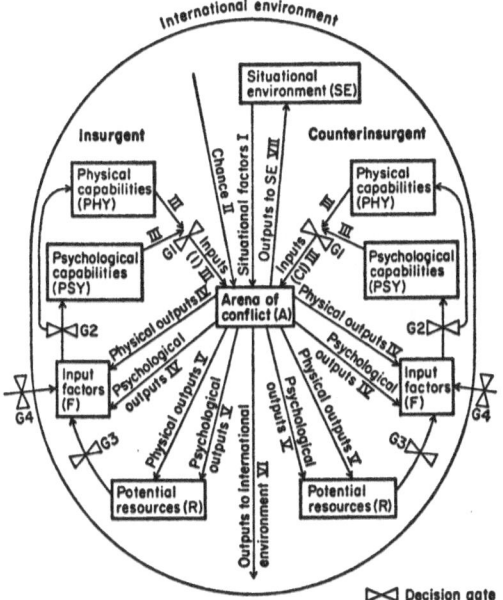

Fig. 3.

NOTATION: Y(I) denotes that the Y referred to is on the insurgent side of the model. Y(CI) indicates the counterinsurgent side, and Y without postscript indicates either that the factor is common to both sides or is being used to refer to Y as a class.

insurgent capabilities (physical and psychological) III (I); (4) counterinsurgent capabilities (physical and psychological) III (CI).

The situational environment (SE), consists of both political and physical factors. The term *political factors* refers to the situational variables which differentiate civil, anticolonial, and antioccupation insurgencies. As suggested in Chapter II, inputs, outputs and decision-making (control) patterns will all be influenced by the nature of the insurgent-counterinsurgent relationship. Through their influence on the objectives, resources, and vulnerabilities of the parties to the conflict, these variables lead to major differences in strategy and tactics, resource utilization, leadership recruitment, and other inputs.

The physical aspects of the situational environment consist primarily of terrain and climate. These inputs are fixed since they may have a profound influence on the nature of the conflict but do not respond readily to human efforts at control. For example, it would no doubt have benefited the Algerian rebels if they could have had a jungle available for concealment, but there was no way that they could manufacture one. Weather also falls into this category. The monsoon season creates problems for counterinsurgent forces dependent on air power, but those forces are incapable of altering the monsoons. The model does show a feedback loop to the situational environment (VII), however, to indicate that change is at least occasionally possible. Efforts at defoliation in Vietnam provide an example.

Chance (II) is indicated as an input into the arena of conflict because it is present to some extent in almost all human activities. One might refer to it alternatively as luck, a random factor, noise, or the will of the gods. Examples of chance in warfare are numerous. During a routine police raid in Manila, the government forces chanced to round up most of the Huk leadership. Before the battle of Antietam General McClellan chanced upon a copy of Robert E. Lee's battle plans.

The capabilities of the insurgent [III (I)] and the counterinsurgent [III (CI)] generate the capacity of each to operate in the arena of conflict. What are the main types of input into the arena coming from each participant? First, as noted above, each side can take actions generating physical flows and psychological responses. Second, each side is trying to alter the balance of capabilities in its favor. Doing this will require "constructive" actions aimed at increasing its own capabilities and "destructive" actions aimed at reducing the capabilities of the opponent. For convenience, therefore, actions might be classified in accordance with the simple four-cell matrix depicted below.

A given action may, of course, fit into more than a single category. A successful action against enemy troops, for example, might also undermine enemy morale. This example makes it clear that a physical action—an attack in this case—can alter both physical (PHY) and psychological (PSY) capabilities. It is also evident that a psychological operation, such as a propaganda campaign, can also alter both physical and psychological capabilities.

	Constructive Actions	Destructive Actions
Actions producing physical results	Increasing manpower, weaponry, etc.	killing enemy troops, destroying enemy supplies
Actions producing psychologcial results	Improving morale, improving loyalty of population, etc.	undermining morale of enemy troops, trying to alienate population from enemy, etc.

Fig. 4.

Similar actions may have a dissimilar impact upon capabilities depending upon the type of insurgency involved. For example, population control measures aimed at reducing insurgent capabilities, such as the resettling of local populations in Vietnam and Algeria or mass imprisonment of males in areas occupied by Germany in World War II, would have more serious feedback consequences for an indigenous counterinsurgent who needs popular support than for a colonial power or an occupying army that will have already written off the possibility of popular support. Similarly, insurgent use of terror will be less likely to produce adverse popular reaction when aimed at colonial or occupation forces than when aimed at the forces of an indigenous counterinsurgent.

There may be a marked disproportion in the quantity of inputs fed into the area of conflict from the two antagonists, but this fact should not obscure the similarity of the process in each case. Each side will try to alter the relative balance of capabilities in its favor and each side will have some capacity to do so.

OUTPUTS FROM THE CONFLICT ARENA

The interaction of the insurgents and the counterinsurgents in the arena of conflict generates various results or outputs. These outputs will be shaped by the interplay of all the elements feeding into the arena of conflict: chance (II), situational factors (I), the capabilites of each side (III), the way in which the capabilities are employed (G1), and the interaction and conflict that take place in the arena (A).

Outputs from the conflict arena take the form of influences of a physical or a psychological nature. These influences may affect the basic input factors (F) of either side or the potential resources (R) of either side. In addition, some of the outputs from the arena of conflict will feed back into the international environment (VI).

POTENTIAL RESOURCES (R)

The term *potential resource* (R) is used to refer to a resource over which one of the contestants has a degree of control and may be able to utilize at a later date. This may be a resource a contestant has chosen not to try to use, such as a manpower resource which the government has not exploited. It may be a resource which a contestant has not learned how to use or determined whether it is worth the effort necessary to employ it.

Actions can be taken by a participant to increase the potential resources available to him or to diminish those available to the enemy. These actions may be designed to generate a flow of physical resources or of psychological responses.

Figure 3 indicates that the box representing potential resources (R) is connected to that representing input factors (F) by a decision gate (G3). The gate signifies that a decision is required before potential resources (R) can be mobilized and transformed into input factors (F) and fed into the arena of conflict as physical (PHY) or psychological capabilities (PSY).

BASIC INPUT FACTORS (F)

Six input factors (F) must be available to each side if it is to carry on the struggle: manpower, population utilization, intelligence, leadership, organization, and logistics.[1] These factors, and the relationships among them, will be discussed in detail in chapter IV. The input factors differ from potential resources in that they are already mobilized for use.

The basic input factors may be fed from three sources: from the arena of conflict (A), from the pool of potential resources

---

1. These same factors were discussed in Chapter II. In that chapter manpower and population utilization were treated together as were leadership and organization.

(R), and from the international environment. The first of these is usually the most important. Since these input factors provide the basis for a participant's capabilities, efforts to alter the balance of capabilities are naturally directed toward them. For example, when the British forces in Malaya sought to cut off the Malayan guerrillas from their food supplies, they were striking at the insurgents' logistical input factor, the point at which they considered the insurgents to be most vulnerable. The leaders of the insurgent movement, which will be typically weaker than the government in its military capabilities, will strike at those basic inputs where the government is weakest, such as, perhaps, intelligence.

PHYSICAL AND PSYCHOLOGICAL CAPABILITIES (PHY AND PSY)
Basic input factors are not the same thing as capabilities. The input factors (F) are the raw material, so to speak, from which capabilities (PHY and PSY) are manufactured. Before the manufacturing process can get under way, however, decisions have to be made concerning the kinds of capabilities to be produced and the desired amount of each. The decision gate (G2) shown on the graphic model indicates the necessity for decisions on these matters.

When decisions are made, they are implemented by varying the mix of basic inputs. The basic input factors can be blended in a wide variety of ways to produce different mixes of capabilities. For example, if the counterinsurgent leadership decided to increase sharply its capability for civic action, it would have to alter the blend of input factors (F) (manpower, logistics, leadership) that had previously been designed to produce a maximum combat potential. Chapter IV offers a discussion of the way in which input factors can be substituted for one another to achieve various blends.

STRATEGY AND TACTICS (G1)
The extent of the capabilities available to each side and the way that those capabilities are utilized in the arena of conflict will usually determine the victor in the struggle between insurgent and counterinsurgent. Capabilities do not employ themselves automatically in the conflict arena however. There are likely to be many ways in which a given set of capabilities

can be employed, and decisions have to be made concerning the way that they *will be* employed.

It will be seen in the graphic presentation of the model that capabilities flow into the conflict arena through a decision gate (G1). This gate signifies the necessity of making decisions on the employment of capabilities in the arena. These decisions are governed by decision-makers' perceptions of the respective capabilities of the two sides and their tactical and strategic objectives. Each side will make continuing strategic and tactical decisions concerning the employment of its capabilities in the arena of conflict in pursuit of its goals.

With the flow of capabilities into the arena of conflict, as modified by each side's selection and employment of strategy and tactics, the loop has been completed, and the discussion of the operational model is back to the point at which it began.

A CYCLE OF THE MODEL

Having completed a discussion of the elements in the operational model, it might help to clarify the working of the model to trace an example through an entire cycle.

A preliminary caveat is in order. Thus far the discussion of the model has ignored the element of time. The flows that have been depicted do take time, however. In some cases, lags will be of great significance. Today's potential resources (R) are not necessarily tomorrow's capabilities (PHY or PSY). It is one thing to decide to mobilize thousands of civilians into an army and quite another thing to actually do it. In addition, there is usually noise and confusion in the channels through which the flows move. Events may occur with no one being sure what they are or what they mean. Combatants on both sides may leave a battlefield demoralized from mutual perceptions of defeat or buoyed by the belief that they had been victorious. In short, while the flows depicted in the model represent the basic processes at work, it would be naïve to expect that developments in an actual conflict would be so rapid, clear-cut, and certain.

A description of the cycle might begin at the point where inputs enter the arena of conflict (A). We shall trace a typical insurgent operation—the ambush of a counterinsurgent convoy. First, the insurgent employs some of his capabilities [PHY (I) and PSY (I)], for example, a company of hardened guerrillas. Their plan (G1) is to attack the convoy at a certain point of the road. The counterinsurgent, too, has capabilities [PHY (CI) and PSY (CI)] employed in this operation—the men and equipment of his convoy. They also plan to move from point A to point B, taking precautions against ambush. The situational environment (SE) plays a role too. Perhaps it is raining, thus hampering the counterinsurgent's air support, and the terrain is heavily wooded and rough. This creates a variety of good ambush sites (I). However the counterinsurgent has modified the environment somewhat (VII) by clearing a swath on both sides of the road, making ambush more difficult. Chance (II) may intrude. A guerrilla accidentally steps on a mine, thus revealing the ambush, or an accompanying counterinsurgent armored vehicle turns back due to mechanical failure. Whatever the precise situation, the stage is now set.

We enter the arena of conflict (A) as the first shot is fired. Perhaps the insurgents are completely successful and destroy the convoy and its complement of soldiers. Perhaps the counterinsurgents are prepared and deal the insurgents a sharp reversal. Whatever the precise nature of the conflict, certain results emerge from the conflict arena. Some results of an insurgent victory might be the following.

a. an improvement in insurgent morale (a psychological developmental output [IV (I)]
b. the capture of useful weapons (a physical developmental output) [IV (I)]
c. the destruction of counter-insurgent material (a physical destructive output [IV (CI)]
d. a deterioration in counter-insurgent morale (a psychological destructive output [IV (CI)]

The results may be reversed. Or there may be a mixed bag of pluses and minuses for each side. At any rate, results flow from the action, and they have an impact upon the basic input factors for both sides. Potential resources (R) of the antagonists may also be affected. The ability or inability of the counterinsurgents to keep the road open may greatly affect the status of areas along the road. With the road closed, the insurgents may take over a previously contested region and thereby increase their potential resources [V (I)]. Or, if the road is opened, the counterinsurgents may be able to control a greater area than had previously been possible [V (CI)].

Each antagonist may also seek to use the outcome of the recent action to modify the relative balance of capabilities. The insurgents may exploit the newly won territory [R (I)] to increase basic input factors such as more troops and better intelligence. The counterinsurgents, if victorious, might take the occasion to bring in more troops and increase the security of the area [R (CI)].

The results of the action may affect potential resources (R) and will probably affect the basic input factors (F). This means that physical (PHY) and psychological (PSY) capabilities will also be affected. In addition, the strategy and tactics (G1) adhered to by both sides may be altered. The insurgents may decide to place greater emphasis upon ambushes and may decide to try to close the road altogether. The counterinsurgent commander may place greater reliance on armored escorts or may be moved to organize a search and destroy the mission directed against the insurgents. We are now back to our starting point, having completed a military action and having traced some of its possible ramifications through the system.

CONTROL SYSTEMS

The control systems of the insurgents and the counterinsurgents are symmetrical. However what occurs in equivalent boxes on the two sides may be different, and the relative weight of the various factors in determining decisions may be thoroughly asymmetrical. Asymmetry in the evaluation of factors may also be associated with the type of insurgency involved. The control system of the counterinsurgent may be a colonial power, a national government faced with overthrow, or a military command occupying conquered territory while responsible to its home government. The varying circumstances of these different control systems will inevitably lead to differences in objectives, motivation, and determination, the stakes involved, and the time and attention devoted to the struggle. The control system of each antagonist is depicted in the figure below.

Perhaps the best way to begin an analysis of this schematic diagram of a control system is to think of the entire system as a "black box" and to ask what constitutes inputs into the system and what emerges as outputs. On the input side, we find primarily perceptions of the course of the conflict. These perceptions may be relatively accurate in some cases, but, as perceptions, they are always bound to introduce some element of distortion. The actual events in the field are filtered through a perceptual screen and the antagonists act on the basis of these filtered results. The output of the control system is a continuing set of decisions concerning strategy and tactics (G1), the desired blend of input factors (G2), and whether and how potential resources ought to be utilized (G3). The control system as a whole, therefore, is a means for converting a stream of perceptions concerning the conflict into a stream of relevant decisions concerning present and future behavior.

RELATIVE CAPABILITIES ANALYSIS (RA)

The first step toward the formulation of strategic plans for the conflict by either side is the analysis of the relative capabilities (RA) of the two sides. This analysis must concern itself not only with present capabilities but probable lines of future development. There are three main elements which are relevant to this analysis.

a. the assessment of one's own capabilities, including other capability requirements, basic input factors, and potential resources (C)
b. the opposition's capabilities, basic input factors, and potential resources (EC)
c. an estimate of the enemy's will and determination (ED)

Each of these elements is subject to a substantial degree of error in measurement. When the three are taken together, it is not surprising that the analysis of relative capabilities (RA) often falls wide of the mark. Nevertheless the relative capabilities analysis does represent the more rational part of the decision process. It is the point at which each antagonist determines the nature of the situation that it faces.

The views of either side concerning the stakes (ST) in question are derived from one's perception of the relationship of one's own goals (G) to the goals of the opponent (EG). The stakes for a participant may be thought of as the gains that he would derive from victory relative to the losses that would be associated with defeat.

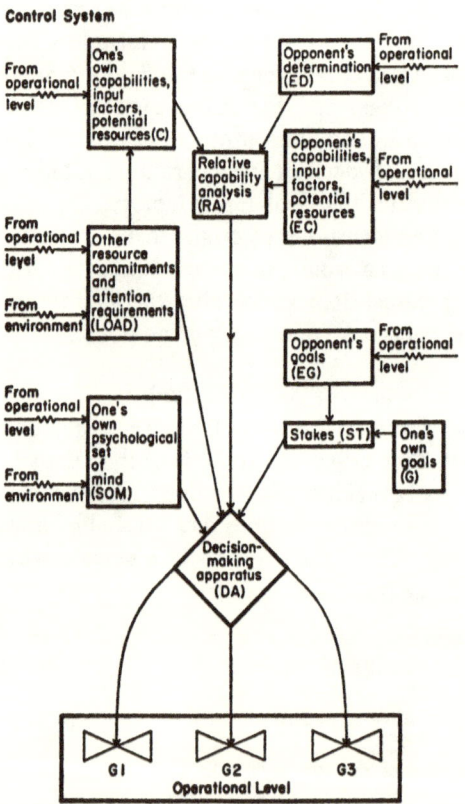

Fig. 5.

The counterinsurgent will define his stakes primarily in terms of what defeat will mean since victory will probably involve little more than the continuance of the status quo. If the insurgent is perceived as seeking limited reforms or simply a role in the government, the stakes for which the counterinsurgents are playing are less than if the insurgents planned to turn the government out of office and execute its leading figures. Similarly, an indigenous regime will be more agitated about the overthrow of the existing political and social system than a colonial power will be about the loss of a distant territory.

For the insurgents the stakes are likely to be high, since victory will probably mean the exercise of state powers, and defeat may mean death. The counterinsurgent leadership should be aware that they can alter the stakes for the insurgents by their own actions. For example, if they promise to execute all the leading insurgents, then the threatened insurgents will be prepared to pay virtually any price for victory. On the other hand, if the government offers amnesty to the insurgent leaders, some of them may be induced to surrender when the situation becomes difficult.

PSYCHOLOGICAL SET (SOM)

The truly rational decision maker would not be governed by passion or emotion in making decisions, but all ordinary mortals are prey to the influence of nonrational psychological factors. For example, if a foe is deeply hated, decisions concerning behavior toward that foe are likely to incorporate a nonrational element. The fact that sacrifices may already have been made in a struggle is also likely to introduce a nonrational element. It may lead to a solemn resolve that those who have died shall not have died in vain. To be sure, the sacrifices of one side in every war are likely to be in vain since someone must lose the war. This consideration is akin to the economists' *sunk-cost fallacy*. The personal characteristics of leaders —including determination, flexibility, willingness to compromise—also contribute to the psychological set (SOM) of the participants.

DECISION-MAKING APPARATUS (DA)

Each participant in the struggle seeks to alter the balance of capabilities in its favor in order to achieve its ultimate objectives. The factors influencing the way this is to be done are four: the relative capabilities analysis, the stakes involved in the struggle, the psychological set of the decision makers, and the over-all load on the administrative organization.

The actual decisions are generated at this stage by the decision-making apparatus (DA). This is the mechanism—and it may be organized many ways—which produces the decision that activates the three decision gates of the operational model (G1, G2, G3). Here decisions will be made concerning when and how potential resources are to be converted into basic input factors (G3), the particular way in which the basic input factors are to be blended to produce capabilities (G2), and the tactics and strategy to be used in deploying capabilities in the arena of conflict (G1).

For maximum efficiency the decision-making process should coordinate all three types of decisions in accordance with an over-all strategic plan. As a practical matter, however, these different types of decisions are often not fully co-ordinated. The men concerned with strategy and tactics may emphasize population control and suppression while those concerned with building increased psychological capabilities may be emphasizing good relations with the populace. A second difficulty is the existence of time lags and noise in the channels that pass the decisions of the top authorities down to lower levels. Orders may be delayed, never received, misinterpreted, or ignored.

A third problem involves administrative load. Decision making occurs in an environment in which matters other than the military struggle are usually competing for the attention of the decision maker. The insurgent leader, for example, may have to deal with the collection of taxes, the maintenance of order, and the provision of food in areas the movement controls. Counterinsurgent leaders are likely to be burdened far more. They must normally deal with the full range of problems confronting an ongoing government. For a colonial power, the conduct of war against an insurgent may comprise a small part of the total decision-making load. A government conducting a large war may be able to give little attention to suppressing partisan insurgents in occupied areas. For example, German occupation forces in Yugoslavia were often hampered in combatting partisans because of the low priority given to their efforts and the resulting difficulty in getting an appropriate allocation of resources. A control system's control will often, therefore be less than perfect. Nonetheless, it will strive, if rational, to alter the capabilities balance in a favorable direction.

A CYCLE OF A CONTROL SYSTEM

To trace the working of a control system, it might be useful to return to the earlier example of an insurgent ambush and note the response of the counterinsurgent control system to the results of that action. Reports on the action would provide a basis for assessing its effects on the counterinsurgent's capabilities, basic input factors, and potential resources (C). If the action ended in a defeat for the counterinsurgents, it might produce the following results.

a. Loss of men and material would reduce the basic input factors—manpower and logistics.
b. Inability of the counterinsurgents to cope with this type attack might lead to a sharp scaling down in estimates of the physical capabilities of the counterinsurgents.
c. Defeat might lower the morale of the survivors, thus lowering the psychological capabilities of the counterinsurgents.
d. Defeat might cause the counterinsurgent forces to appear less formidable to the populace and hence reduce their psychological capability.

For the insurgent, on the other hand, there would be numerous pluses.

The capabilities balance has been altered as a consequence of the action, and the counterinsurgent is likely to conclude that he must do something to restore the situation and to alter the new capabilities balance in his favor (RA). Perhaps, after their triumph, the insurgents began to loot and burn the homes of government supporters in the region near where the action took place. This new development would indicate that the insurgent's goals (EG) have escalated and that reconciliation has become less likely. Furthermore, the attack in territory that had hitherto been quiet may indicate to the counterinsurgent that he cannot allow the insurgents to roam freely in this area but must either drive them out or destroy them. The stakes have been raised, inhibitions have been thrown off, and the psychology of the decision makers (SOM) has been altered.

Now the counterinsurgent generates his plans for altering the capabilities balance. At the strategic and tactical gate (G1), he decides the lost territory must not go uncontested. Hence, helicopter assaults are ordered on various villages to inhibit insurgent exploitation. Since the action has revealed inadequacies in the counterinsurgent's capability mix, decisions are made to improve the mobility and aggressiveness of the troops (G2). Further, since the escalation of the conflict demonstrated the seriousness of the situation, new taxes are levied and more troops mustered into the army as the counterinsurgent girds for the next round (G3).

The working of the counterinsurgency control system has now been traced through a complete cycle. The process would be similar if the working of the insurgent control system were examined. It must be emphasized again that the information fed into a control system is filtered through a perceptual screen and is also likely to be distorted by lags, noise, and sometimes outright deception (e.g., junior officer falsifying combat outcomes).

ESCALATION

Escalation means an increase in the magnitude and virulence of the conflict. To have escalation, at least one side must decide either to utilize its existent capabilities more intensively or to acquire and employ greater capabilities.

MOTIVATIONS FOR ESCALATION

Given the ability, the insurgent leaders might escalate for several reasons.

a. They may believe the present level of conflict is so low it holds no promise of victory.
b. They may conclude, as a result of a relative capabilities analysis, that they can stand the strain of escalation better than the counterinsurgents can. If the counterinsurgents are trying to maintain a multiple of insurgent strength, say eight or nine to one, a net addition of one unit to insurgent strength would force the counterinsurgents to add eight or nine units.
c. The insurgents might conclude that if they escalated the conflict the total potential resources available to the counterinsurgents would soon be committed, and the ratio of insurgent to counterinsurgent forces could not fail to improve.
d. After examining the goals and stakes of the opponent the in-

surgents might conclude that they should escalate further since the counterinsurgents would be unwilling to (for example, if the counterinsurgents represented a colonial or occupying power) and hence would have to make concessions or sue for peace.
e. The insurgents might increase the level of their activity because counterinsurgent escalation left them no alternative.

In other circumstances the insurgents might be wise to avoid escalation or even to seek to de-escalate the conflict. For example, the leaders of a movement might be well advised to operate at a sufficiently low level of activity during the early stage of their movement to avoid drawing a full-scale counterinsurgent effort from the government. Such an effort might be fatal to the movement. If the movement were operating at a high level of activity and was nevertheless slowly being crushed, the leaders might wish to consider a sharp reduction in the level of effort in the hope of encouraging a corresponding reduction in effort by the counterinsurgents.

Guevara advised revolutionaries to adjust the level of insurgent activities to keep it slightly below the all-out response threshold of the counterinsurgent. It may be difficult for the insurgent to locate this threshold, but an approximation is probably better than nothing. The insurgent should be aware that the location of this threshold may shift during the course of a protracted conflict. As a movement grows, however, a time may come when Guevara's advice can no longer be followed. If it is to continue growing, it must inevitably precipitate an all-out response from the counterinsurgent.

The counterinsurgents may also have reasons for wanting to escalate the conflict. In the early stages of an insurgency, the movement is likely to be very vulnerable: leaders are still learning their jobs; training and logistics arrangements are likely to be poor; manpower may be inadequate; and the flow of intelligence is also likely to be inadequate. It would be a rational course of action for the counterinsurgent to overreact to the insurgency and to crush it at the outset. However, the very vulnerability of the movement causes its threat to appear minimal, and the response of the counterinsurgent is therefore likely to be minimal. Furthermore, when a government is faced by a civil insurgency, it is usually loathe to acknowledge that a serious threat really exists and will incline in the direction of underreacting rather than overreacting.

There are good reasons for each side to consider escalation a desirable strategy. Tracing the escalation of an insurgency through the entire model serves a twofold purpose: exploration of the phenomenon of escalation and demonstration of the efficacy of our model for describing the complex interrelationships of insurgent situations.

THE PROCESS OF ESCALATION: AN EXAMPLE

In this section the working of the operational model and the control system model will be illustrated by the use of an example, an example of escalation. A number of flows move through these models simultaneously, but for purposes of exposition the process has been simplified. To have a point of entry into the model, it will be assumed arbitrarily that the insurgents have decided upon a significant escalation of effort. The consequences of this action will be traced until a cycle has been completed.

The insurgent control system has decided to increase the level of its operations in a province close to the counterinsurgent capital city. Three types of interrelated decisions have to be made concurrently. One type decision (G2) concerns the input factors necessary for the escalation. If there is to be an escalation of effort, it will require increases in certain inputs: manpower, logistical support, and intelligence. Significant changes in leadership and population utilization policies are also planned. A new mix of input factors is designed to provide for the increased capabilities needed.

A second type decision (G3) concerns the mobilization of potential resources. If inputs are to be increased to generate greater capabilities, mobilization of additional potential resources is required. Therefore, it is decided to broaden the recruitment effort, expand the training program, develop new sources of supply, and to improve the insurgent intelligence-gathering apparatus in the province.

The third type decision (G1) involves strategy and tactics. The insurgent leaders decide to marshall what troops they can to make surprise attacks on government troops in their barracks in a number of towns. At the very least, the insurgents believe, their successes will humiliate the government and have an impact upon public opinion, and their successes might set in motion a chain of events leading to the government's downfall.

The insurgent plan begins to be executed. The physical and psychological capabilities of the insurgents, applied in accordance with their decisions on strategy and tactics, become inputs into the arena of conflict. The counterinsurgent input (III-CI) consists of military garrisons in several major towns plus various unimaginative policies with regard to the population. As noted earlier, situational factors comprise one of the inputs into the arena of conflict. The terrain in the province is wooded, which is to the advantage of the insurgents. A fairly elaborate system of roads, however, is advantageous to the counterinsurgents. A final input into the arena of conflict is chance. Chance plays a role in the unfolding of events in the arena of conflict because the commanding officer of the government forces in the province proves to be a singularly inept individual. Several months earlier he personally assured the president that the insurgents were no more than a handful of bandits and posed no real security threat. When reports of a planned attack came to him, he rejected them out of hand.

The insurgent attacks were well planned, and tactical surprise was complete. The attacks were simultaneous, followed the same pattern, and were made at night. Barracks were set afire, and soldiers were machine-gunned as they tried to flee the burning buildings. By dawn organized government forces had ceased to exist in the province. For the time, at least, the insurgents controlled the province. They proceeded to imprison some government officials and execute others. The insurgent organization, that had operated clandestinely to this point, came into the open and began to function in a limited way as the *de facto* government of the province. A large-scale propaganda program was instituted to persuade the populace of the villages and towns to give their allegiance to the insurgents.

Insurgent inputs into the arena of conflict interact with the other inputs and result in certain outputs. Some of these outputs affect the insurgents themselves and others affect the counterinsurgents. On the constructive side, the potential resources available to the insurgents increase sharply as the insurgents begin to exercise control over the province. The constructive psychological output from the arena of conflict takes the form of improved morale among the insurgents and the improved standing of the insurgent movement among villagers and townspeople. The only destructive psychological output derives from the bitterness of a portion of the populace because of the damage to their homes and farms as a consequence of the fighting. There is a destructive physical output because of casualties suffered and equipment lost.

A number of destructive physical outputs from the arena of conflict affect the government. Garrison forces (an input factor for the counterinsurgents) have been destroyed. The government has lost control of the food production in the province, and this is a serious matter since the capital city is dependent to an extent upon those foodstuffs. Loss of control of the province also reduced the opportunity for recruitment of young men into the armed forces. The destructive psychological outputs for the counterinsurgents are scarcely less important. The prestige of the government and of the military forces suffered greatly. The populace was exposed to the arguments of the insurgents over an extended period of time, and many appear ready to co-operate with the insurgents either from fear or from conviction.

On the balance, the outputs from the arena of conflict following the insurgent escalation are highly favorable to the insurgents. The counter-insurgent control system receives information about events in the province and evaluates that information. A new relative capability analysis (RA) is made. The counterinsurgent control system perceives that the government's capabilities, its basic inputs, and its potential resources have all been adversely affected. It also perceives the gains of the insurgents (EC). In much the same way that the capabilities of the insurgents had previously been underestimated, they now tend to be exaggerated. Once again the raw information received by the control system is fairly accurate, but the system introduces a significant element of perceptual distortions (SOM).

The government reassesses the determination of the insurgents (ED) and finds it greater than anticipated. It also begins to perceive, in a different way, the stakes involved (ST). The opponents' goal (EG) is now correctly perceived to be the overthrow of the government. As a consequence of events in the province and the control system's analysis of those events, the government now concludes: (1) that it is not dealing with bandit gangs but with an organized and growing insurgency; (2) that the insurgent movement is determined and well led; and (3) that its capabilities are far greater than had been realized.

Until the attack on the province, the insurgent offensive remained below the threshold at which the government would perceive itself as threatened. Now that threshold has been passed, and the government's reaction is one of alarm. In the past the government had been content to react locally and on a small scale to what it regarded as relatively inconsequential acts of banditry. Now its goal with regard to the insurgency becomes more comprehensive, namely, destruction of the movement.

Decisions are made to give effect to this new goal. Potential resources are examined, and it is decided to make a sharp increase in the number of men conscripted. Aid is sought, and received, from a foreign country, thus constituting an input (G4) from the international environment. The mix of basic input factors is altered to give a different output. Strategy and tactics are modified in the light of the new situation. Changes are made in the leadership of the military forces, and the commanding officer in the province is retired in favor of a younger and more aggressive officer. A decision is made to alter the stakes for the individual insurgent, and it is announced that all insurgents who are captured will be executed in the field. The president also announces that the properties of those who collaborate with the insurgents are subject to confiscation. In short, the counterinsurgent control system responds to insurgent escalation of the conflict by organizing a pronounced counterinsurgent escalation.

These actions provide a new counterinsurgent input into the arena of conflict. A series of attacks are mounted on towns held by the insurgents. These inputs generate a new series of physical outputs. The towns are recaptured by the government forces with relative ease, substantial quantities of insurgents' weapons and supplies are seized, and several prominent insurgent leaders lose their lives in the fighting. The psychological outputs are also important. The insurgent movement ceases to look like the wave of the future to many villagers, and they adopt a more cautious attitude toward collaboration with the insurgents. The government's threat of property confiscation is taken very seriously. Within the insurgent movement morale drops, the desertion rate rises, and the flow of new recruits into the movement almost ceases.

The insurgent control system perceives and evaluates the physical and psychological outputs from the arena of conflict. After considerable soul searching, the insurgent leaders acknowledge that the attack on the province was premature and ill conceived. They acknowledge that this action has aroused the government and that their own forces are not yet capable of engaging government units in the field. They decide to return to hit-and-run tactics, albeit on a larger scale than previously, and to build for the future. They console themselves with the thought that they have demonstrated the vulnerability of the government forces and have put their movement on the map.

Appropriate orders are given by the insurgent control system, and the actions that are taken in consequence provide a series of new insurgent inputs into the arena of conflict. Since this example of escalation began with a series of insurgent inputs, the cycle that was to be examined has now been completed.

CHAPTER IV

INPUTS, OUTPUTS, AND SUBSTITUTABILITY

INPUT FACTORS

▬▬▬ Chapter II discussed the principal types of insurgency and noted some key differences among those types, and chapter III presented a model of the functioning of insurgent movements. This chapter will be devoted to an analysis of feaures that are common to all insurgencies—be they anticolonial, civil, or in opposition to an invading army—and without which an insurgency would cease to exist. Six basic input factors will be noted.

   a. leadership
   b. organization
   c. manpower
   d. intelligence
   e. logistics
   f. population utilization

LEADERSHIP

Leadership is the element that weaves together the other inputs and fashions them into a viable movement. It is difficult to say what successful insurgent leadership involves because so much depends upon the environment in which the insurgent leader and his movement are to operate. Personal characteristics that might be valuable in one environment might prove to be a handicap in another. Indeed, different leadership characteristics may be called for from the leadership at different points in the evolution of a single movement. If the characteristics of a handful of insurgent leaders are examined —men such as T. E. Lawrence, Mao Tse-tung, Fidel Castro, Ho Chi Minh, Che Guevara, and the young Tito—it is apparent there is room for considerable variation in personality.

Of the many qualities that may be desirable in an insurgent

leader, only a few can safely be termed essential. The leader must be adaptable. One of the keys to the success of an insurgency lies in its capacity to adapt, but a movement can exhibit adaptability only if its leaders are themselves adaptable. In addition the leader must be a reasonably good organizer or must, at least, be able to use the organizational talents of others. Finally, an effective leader must have the capacity to win and hold the support of many kinds of people.

There are a number of functions that the insurgent leader must perform (or have performed) if the movement is to prosper. He must develop a body of politico-military doctrine to guide junior officers and the rank and file in their activities. He must take care of important managerial functions—organize a communications system and logistic support, develop training facilities and doctrine, organize an intelligence apparatus, and recruit followers. He must make a continuing series of decisions concerning how input factors are to be combined and the type of outputs that the movement should seek to produce. He must function as both a political and a military leader. It may be desirable to have apolitical leaders in regular armies, but an apolitical insurgent leader is a likely candidate for early defeat. The leader must also provide the movement with an over-all ideology. The content of the ideology will vary with the type of insurgency and with the immediate circumstances in which the insurgency erupted. It is easier to elaborate an ideology in support of an anticolonial insurgency or in opposition to an invading army than to develop the kind of ideology needed for a civil insurgency. If it is to provide the power and thrust for a civil insurgency, an ideology would probably need to indict the existing social, political, and economic system, explain why conditions are intolerable, argue that no improvement can be expected until the present government is overthrown, offer convincing reasons for believing that the government can be overthrown, describe the improvements to be expected if the insurgents gain power, and, finally, move people to action.

ORGANIZATION

An insurgent movement cannot come into existence nor persist through time unless there is organization, division of labor, and co-ordination of effort. In the earliest stages of a movement's development its organizational structure may be very simple. For example, during the retreat of the Red Army after the Nazi invasion of the Soviet Union, Stalin was able to do little more than call for the establishment of partisan groups and issue a few general guidelines for their operation. Subsequent to his call, a number of local partisan groups were organized. They functioned in a relatively autonomous way for a number of months before the Soviet leadership was able to establish contact with them and begin to give co-ordinated direction to their efforts. Without organization the efforts of individual insurgent units are not likely to be sustained, and without over-all co-ordination and direction they can have little strategic impact. The fragmentation of the resistance movement in the Netherlands during World War II was one of the factors that prevented it from realizing its full potential.

As an insurgent movement develops its organizational structure must become more complex and elaborate. The demands of logistics, planning, and intelligence create a strong thrust in this direction. If the development of the movement's organizational structure should fail to keep pace with the development of other aspects of the movement, the effectiveness of the movement would be seriously hindered. There is room for variation in the degree of centralization or decentralization existing in a movement, and there is room for variation in the extent of the division of labor within a movement (intelligence, recruiting, logistics, planning, propaganda). There is also room for variation in the way the political and military functions are related to one another, but in each case organizational arrangements should be adapted to the needs of the movement at the stage of the development it is in and to the special circumstances of the insurgency.

MANPOWER

The recruitment, training, and maintenance of manpower is obviously an essential input factor for any insurgency. Without men to fight, agitate, and organize, there can be no movement. The more serious the general malaise in the society, the greater the number of potential recruits for the insurgency. A variety of factors will influence the extent to which potential recruits can be converted into actual recruits.

If the insurgent ideology sets forth attractive goals and can draw upon the sentiments that are apt to be associated with nationalism, class struggle, and political and economic modernization, this will help attract recruits. One of the difficulties faced by the counterinsurgents is that the gap between ideology and actual behavior is easily apparent because they hold office. The insurgents do not suffer from this disadvantage. Since they do not hold power, their pretensions cannot as easily be contrasted with their performance. The caliber of the leadership and the charisma of the individual leader will have a bearing on recruitment. Similarly, recruitment will be affected by the general prospects of the movement and the immediate success which it may be enjoying. When a movement is suffering setbacks, recruitment is likely to drop off sharply, and the rate of desertion may begin to climb.

Insurgents can be, and often are, recruited from many walks of life—government troops, bandits, students, middle-class intellectuals, workers, peasants. Because of the varied sources of recruits it is relatively easy for counterinsurgents to infiltrate the movement. An individual may join the movement for many reasons. He may be moved by a sense of idealism or driven by a sense of failure. He may be moved by rational calculation or by a desire for personal sacrifice. He may join because he hopes to play an important role in the government to be established after an insurgent victory or because he is at loose ends. He may join because he is an outlaw and needs protection or because he enjoys excitement and violence, and insurgency legitimizes his pursuit of those pleasures. He may wish to topple the government because it is corrupt, inhumane, and undemocratic or because he is a romantic utopian and will be against any government that falls short of an impossible ideal. He may join because he had no real alternative when the insurgents moved into his village and threatened his family. Typically insurgents have varied backgrounds and goals. They are not all bandits, as the government insists, nor all selfless idealists as the leaders of the movement insist.

Once an individual is enrolled as an insurgent, he will undergo training. This training may be brief and haphazard or may be first-rate. Much will depend on where the training is done and on the pressure that the movement is under. The insurgents may be able to set up a training base in a friendly neighboring country or in a safe area in a remote part of their own country. If the insurgents lack a safe base area, training is likely to suffer. If the movement is under heavy pressure, the training period may be short, and most training may be conducted on the job by attaching new recruits to seasoned units in the field.

Usually the insurgents will be short on supplies, in which case training may be conducted without the use of actual weapons. An insurgent movement is usually eager for new recruits, but under certain circumstances its ability to absorb new recruits might be limited by its capacity to equip and arm. However, if a movement has enjoyed enough success to have attracted large number of new recruits, that same success (in the form of ambushes and raids on government depots) may have produced the arms and equipment needed to supply the new recruits.

The training of insurgents will be different in certain respects from the training of recruits in conventional military forces. Political indoctrination may play a major role, while close order drill and the training appropriate to the parade ground will be ignored. Physical conditioning will receive heavy stress as will the capacity to operate under conditions of hunger, fatigue, and pursuit. Heavy emphasis will be laid on the skills of patrolling and scouting and on ways to take advantage of surprise.

The individual may decide to join the movement for any of a large number of reasons, but, once he has joined, the psychology of group reinforcement comes into play. If group loyalty is strong in the unit to which he is attached, the individual will probably share that feeling. Once the group becomes important to him, the likelihood of his defecting, even during a prolonged period of setbacks, is greatly reduced. If group cohesion does not develop, however, morale will remain vulnerable. Defeat may lead to a loss of morale and then to a general reduction in the fighting capacity and discipline of the unit. Discipline in insurgent organizations is largely self-discipline, since the apparatus of formal discipline and courts-martial is absent, and is grounded upon high morale. If morale is weakened, the movement may disintegrate. The individual insurgent may begin to think relatively more of himself and of personal survival and relatively less of the unit and the importance of victory. Aspects of insurgent life that had seemed unimportant may begin to seem important—fatigue, boredom, danger, physical hardship, food shortages, homesickness, the shortcomings of the leader, and doubts about the likelihood of ultimate victory.

INTELLIGENCE

Insurgent movements need intelligence if they are to function effectively. The margin for error is often not very great in their operations, and faulty intelligence can lead to disastrous defeats. Intelligence needs vary, however. The greater the number of semiautonomous units in the field, the greater the intelligence need. The more operations the movement is trying to conduct and the larger the number of locales in which it is trying to operate, the greater will be its need for intelligence. A movement that is in an aggressive expansionist phase will have greater intelligence needs than one that is lying low. The kind of intelligence needed by a movement will also change with the fortunes of the movement. When it is small and operates within narrow geographic confines, it needs information on immediate targets and immediate threats to its safety. This is the kind of information that may be possessed or obtained by the insurgents, their families or friends. As the movement grows, it needs a greater volume of intelligence and it is likely to need a higher proportion of political intelligence to military intelligence.

In certain respects the intelligence task facing the insurgent organization is easier than the task facing the government. Much information is likely to be available in a given locale concerning the location, strength, and plans of government forces in the area. Political intelligence is also likely to be available through the normal operations of the press and the various informal communications networks. In addition, the intelligence capabilities of a movement are likely to grow with its size. As the movement grows it comes into contact with more people, and as it becomes more successful these people will be more willing to co-operate by providing intelligence. This assumes that the movement enjoys a fairly high level of popularity among the people. Intelligence yield and the popular support are often closely linked. As popular support for a movement rises, the flow of intelligence is likely to increase. If popular support declines, there is likely to be a decline in the amount and quality of the intelligence available.

The gathering of intelligence by insurgents is usually carried on by conventional means. To be sure, some use may be made of more specialized techniques such as infiltration of the governmental structure, interrogation of prisoners, examination of captured documents, and monitoring of enemy telephonic communication. The organizational aspects of an insurgency movement are likely to be less elaborate and specialized than those of conventional forces, and the same certainly applies to intelligence. Intelligence is not the exclusive province of a handful of specialists. Instead, every insurgent and supporter of the movement is viewed as a potential source of information. This lack of professionalization may open a broader range of sources of intelligence to the movement, but it may sometimes interfere with the proper evaluation of intelligence gathered by the insurgents.

The insurgents may have a peculiar problem when it comes to accepting and evaluating adverse information. Success is vitally important to the insurgent movement. For some it will be a life and death matter, and the careers and prospects of many others will depend upon it. Furthermore, as noted above, defeats and setbacks may slow recruitment, lower morale, and increase desertion. Defeat, or the prospect of it, may therefore look like the end of the world to the committed insurgent, and for that reason he may have difficulty giving credence to strongly adverse intelligence.

LOGISTICS

An insurgent movement needs a fairly elaborate inventory of food, clothing, weapons, ammunition, and medicine if it is to function effectively. There are many additional items that would be highly desirable, although perhaps not essential, such as communications equipment, mimeograph machines, mosquito netting, and hammocks.

The insurgents have four principal sources of supply: (1) insurgent manufacture; (2) the populace; (3) the counterinsurgents; (4) foreign sources. There may be some insurgent manufacturing while the movement is small, but it is likely to be of a handicraft nature and will be concentrated in items such as canteens, shoes, and very simple weapons. Not until the movement is relatively large and has a secure base area are small factories likely to be built for the production of ammunition, explosives, and small arms.

The populace in the areas in which the insurgents operate may be a source of food and shelter. They may provide these resources because of conviction, because of fear, or as a form of insurance in case the insurgents are successful. The main supplier of weapons and ammunition may be the troops of the government. If the insurgents achieve a degree of standardization of weapons and ammunition, it may be only because they have been successful in their ambushes or their raids on government depots. Weapons may also be obtained from abroad. For example, the Algerians used Czech weapons which came by way of Egypt.

The means used to move weapons and supplies are likely to be highly varied. If there is an extensive border or coastline, it will be difficult for the counterinsurgents to interdict all illicit traffic. Limited quantities of weapons and supplies may enter the country by air-drop, but this method requires a high level of co-ordination between the sender and the receiver. Furthermore, air-drops are likely to attract unwanted attention from government troops. The extent to which truck and wagon transport can be used will normally depend upon the terrain in which fighting is taking place and the extent to which the government forces control the roads and maintain surveillance over them. If the counterinsurgent forces are alert and aggressive, the insurgents may be forced to rely upon human transport and animal transport. For this reason insurgents try to keep their weapons light. They will typically rely upon small arms and, at the most, light mortars.

POPULATION UTILIZATION

The relationship between the population and the insurgents is an important one although the subject is not always well understood. For one thing popular support facilitates access to resources—recruits, food, shelter, weapons, medicine, transportation, couriers, intelligence. If the populace supports an insurgent movement, individuals may be willing to provide hiding places when government troops are in the area and to store food and weapons. This support may improve insurgent morale through the process of psychological reinforcement and may allow the insurgents to levy taxes in the areas they control. In a roundabout way, the populace may protect the insurgents from ruthless action by the counterinsurgents. The counterinsurgents may not be able to get at the insurgents except by harsh action against the entire population in a village, and they may fear to antagonize the villagers further.

It is easier for the insurgents to get popular support in some circumstances than in others. The insurgents will find it easy to mobilize support in a country that has been invaded or occupied and relatively easy in a country in a colonial status. They will sometimes find it difficult to arouse support for a civil insurgency. Such support as exists may center in a particular region or in a racial or religious group. For example, in the case of the Malayan insurgency much of the support for the movement came from the impoverished portion of the Chinese minority. If they can, the insurgents will normally try to build a broader basis for support than would be afforded by a purely regional or ethnic appeal. One of the reasons for the success of the Viet Minh in their struggle against the French in Indo China was their ability to build and maintain a base of support that included peasants, middle-class intellectuals, and Buddhists and members of other religious sects. This patchwork of alliances was held together by religious, nationalist, and social protest sentiments.

Wide support can be generated by a broad-based coalition, but a "united front" of this kind is apt to be highly vulnerable to centrifugal forces. For example, during the Algerian insurgency a major split appeared between the FLN (National Liberation Front) and the MNA (Algerian National Movement). As victory approaches and as the factions within a movement begin to direct their attention more toward the political arrangements to be established after the fighting stops, the tendency toward factionalism increases sharply.

The way that the insurgents behave toward the populace will influence the way they come to be viewed by the populace. They should try to conduct their affairs with a minimum disruption of peasant life and should avoid harshness, brutality, and thievery in dealing with the peasants. It will be helpful if they can be of positive aid to the peasants—with harvests, for example. The contrast between such behavior and the behavior of the government troops may be helpful to the insurgents.

A population is not, of course, a single homogeneous mass. It is a composite of elements with different values, beliefs, aspirations, and ways of life. When the insurgents seek support, each of these groups may present special problems. Some elements may be moved by the appeals of the insurgents while others are neutral, apathetic, or even hostile. The insurgents might offer inducements to the apathetic or the neutral while dealing harshly with the hostile. The leaders of insurgent movements have, on numerous occasions, chosen to use terror selectively against village leaders to discourage collaboration with the government. Occasionally the use of terror has been broadened to include entire hamlets and villages in an area, as in the case of the North Vietnamese Catholic villages or the experimental fortified hamlets in South Vietnam. Terror may of course be used in a still broader way in an effort to frighten a population and induce a compliant attitude. The holding and execution of hostages by the Nazi armies during World War II provides an example of the mass use of terror.

Are there circumstances in which it might be reasonable to use terror against elements in the population, or is that always a mistake? If "winning the hearts and minds" of the people is a primary objective of the insurgents, the use of terror is not likely to contribute to its achievement. How important is popularity to an insurgent movement? It is sometimes assumed, more often tacitly than explicitly, that the success of an insurgency is directly related to its popularity with the people and inversely related to the government's popularity with the people.[1]

1. For a stimulating discussion of insurgency and popular support see the third chapter of Charles Wolf, Jr., *United States Policy and the Third World* (Boston: Little, Brown and Co., 1967).

It has become part of the conventional wisdom concerning insurgency to emphasize the vital nature of popularity. Nevertheless, even on the face of it, there seems to be some question. One recalls, for example, the observation by T. E. Lawrence, apropos his experience in Arabia during the First World War, that an insurgency can be carried on by 2 percent of the population if the remainder of the population is passive and indifferent. Apparently Lawrence felt that widespread popularity was not essential, provided the population was not supporting the counterinsurgents either. It is also easy to recall a number of insurgencies, such as Castro's movement in Cuba, that enjoyed only minimal popularity during their early stages. The Communist-led insurgency in Greece following World War II also survived for several years despite a relatively low level of popular support.

The importance of popularity to an insurgent movement needs to be re-examined and rethought. If movements can get under way and survive without a high level of popular support, popularity is obviously not essential. The absence of popularity would not necessarily mean the demise of a movement, and the presence of popularity would not guarantee its success.

ATTITUDES AND BEHAVIOR

If popularity is not essential to the success of a movement, why is population utilization included as one of the essential input factors in an insurgency? The question draws attention to one of the confusions that has permeated much of the discussion of the subject of insurgency—the failure to distinguish clearly between attitudes of the population on the one hand and behavior on the other. One of the sources of the confusion has lain in the widespread use of the term *popular support*. The term includes both attitude and behavior and hence fosters ambiguity. It implies popularity in the use of the word *popular*, and yet the word *support* can be interpreted, and sometimes is interpreted, to refer to supportive behavior. The term *population utilization* used in this chapter refers solely to behavior and never to attitudes.

If it is important to distinguish between attitudes and behavior in analyzing the success of the insurgents, it is no less important in examining the fortunes of the counterinsurgents.

Programs designed to improve the position of the government in the countryside may not produce the results expected. For example, economic and social development programs supported by the government may create favorable attitudes among the villagers and yet lead to an increased flow of resources to the insurgents. The explanation for the seeming paradox is not hard to find. These programs increase the disposable income of the villagers and hence expand the pool of village resources on which the insurgents can draw. The insurgents may respond to the improved economic circumstances of the villages by demanding greater payments from the villagers in return for the promise of safety and protection.[2] Villagers do not need to be active supporters of an insurgent movement to be willing to make an accommodation with it. They may favor the government but feel that safety and prudence dictate co-operation with the insurgents. It would be quite possible, therefore, for the overall position of an insurgent movement to improve while its popularity in the villages declined, and it would be possible for the position of the government to worsen while its popularity increased.

Since behavior and attitudes can vary independently, it is worth examining the various ways in which they can be combined. Setting aside all refinements of degree, the attitudes of a segment of the population toward the insurgents may be favorable, neutral, or unfavorable. Their behavior toward the insurgents may also be favorable, neutral or unfavorable. This allows the construction of the following matrix.

		ATTITUDES		
		Favorable	Neutral	Unfavorable
B E H A V I O R	Favorable	1	2	3
	Neutral	4	5	6
	Unfavorable	7	8	9

Fig. 1.

2. Ibid., p. 52.

This matrix illustrates the number of possible combinations of attitude and behavior and indicates how much more complex is the question of popular support than has usually been realized. In cell 1 the attitudes of the populace are favorable, and behavior is also favorable. From the point of view of the insurgents, this is the most attractive combination, just as cell 9 would represent the least attractive combination. If cell 1 were not an open option, would the insurgent choose cell 4 next or cell 2? If he chose cell 4, he would enjoy attitudinal support from the populace, but behavior would be neutral. If he chose cell 2, on the other hand, attitudes would be neutral, but behavior would be favorable. The insurgent would normally choose cell 2 rather than cell 4 and would also prefer 3 over 4. The key consideration for the insurgent is not attitude but behavior. Other things being equal, if he must choose between attitude and behavior, he will give preference to the latter. It is preferable for favorable attitudes to be combined with the desired behavior, but behavior remains the dominant concern.

An examination of this matrix will suggest the rationale that may lie behind an insurgent decision to use coercion against a segment of the population. If "winning the hearts and minds" of the populace were all that mattered, the insurgent would never be justified in threatening villagers or using terror against them, for such actions would guarantee the hostility of the villagers. As a practical matter, however, insurgents sometimes do threaten and use coercion and terror. They do so because they want favorable behavior from the villagers and are prepared to use coercion to get it, even if it means loss of popularity. If the attitude of the villagers is already hostile to the insurgents, it will make the decision easier for the insurgents since they do not have any popularity to lose, and any improvement in the behavior of the villagers will be a net gain.

The insurgent wants to utilize the population for his purposes (manpower, cover, intelligence), or failing that, he wants to prevent the counterinsurgents from utilizing the population. He will use persuasion and conditioning to produce attitudes which will predispose their holders toward the desired behavior. If persuasion and conditioning are not capable of producing the desired behavior, then the insurgent will utilize rewards, threats, and punishment. The gap between the attitudes of the populace and the behavior desired by the insurgents may be great. In this case persuasion and conditioning may not be enough by themselves and will have to be supplemented by a program of coercion or control. By and large, the greater the gap, the greater will be the amount of coercion or control needed.

Coercion and control are related but are nevertheless worth distinguishing. As applied to a village, for example, coercion might be sporadic and intermittent whereas control envisages the occupation of a village and the organized domination of its life. If the insurgents have effective control of a village they will not need to resort to violence or terror to get compliant behavior from the villagers. The response of the individual villager to efforts at coercion and control will be a function of his attitudes at the outset, the total complex of rewards and punishments offered by the two competing sides, and the strength of personal traits such as courage and determination.

The role that coercion might play can be analyzed further. Figure 2 indicates a possible distribution of attitudes in the population with regard to both the insurgents and the counterinsurgents.

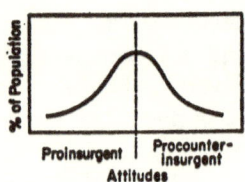

Fig. 2.

This curve suggests a distribution of attitudes approaching the normal. The curve might, of course, be heavily skewed in one direction or the other or might even have a shape such as that in figure 3, indicating a polarization of attitudes. Changes in the distribution of attitudes would be reflected in the changed shape of the curve, but a shifting of the entire curve from left to right or vice versa would indicate a general shift in attitudes. Such changes might reflect the political, economic, or military programs of the insurgents or the counterinsurgents or the success of their psychological operations.

If no other influences intervened, the distribution of behav-

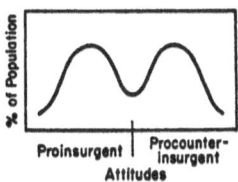

Fig. 3.

ior favorable to the insurgents or to the counterinsurgents would be in accord with the distribution of attitudes. This is illustrated in figure 4.

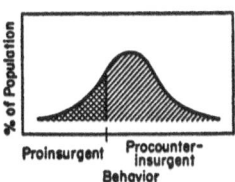

Fig. 4.

Let the insurgents undertake an ambitious program of coercion, however, and the amount of proinsurgent behavior might increase sharply, and the amount of anti-insurgent behavior might decline. Village leaders might conclude that the village would be punished by the insurgents if it continues to aid the government, and they might therefore adopt a neutral stance. Without a notable shift in attitudes, the behavior pattern might change substantially, as indicated in figure 5.

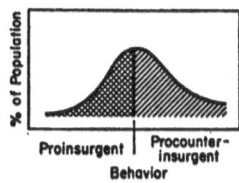

Fig. 5.

SUBSTITUTABILITY

The input factors discussed above are termed essential, because if any one of them were reduced to zero the insurgent movement would cease to exist or would, at least, cease to be effective.[3] An insurgent movement comes into being when basic inputs such as leadership, manpower, intelligence, organization, and logistics are combined. Once it exists, a movement may be thought of as a machine for converting these basic inputs into the outputs that characterize an insurgency. The principal task of the leadership is to make a continuing series of decisions concerning inputs and outputs. The success of the movement will be greatly affected by the skill of the leadership in relating input decisions and output decisions to each other.

The leaders of an insurgency are concerned with producing a product, insurgency. On closer scrutiny, however, this appears not to be a single product but a compound of political and military products—attacks on isolated military units, psychological warfare activities, disruption of communications, terrorism. Each type of output may be regarded as a variable that can be changed with time. These outputs can vary, and the leadership must therefore determine the mix of outputs the movement should produce at a given time.

Since capabilities of an insurgency are limited, a decision to produce more of one type of activity usually implies a decision to produce less of another. If personnel are going to concentrate on blowing up bridges, then they cannot, at the same time, concentrate on improving relations with the people and attacking government units. Assume for the moment that the insurgent leaders must decide on the allocation of scarce resources between two competing uses, political activity (Y) and military activity (X). If all resources were concentrated on political activity, the movement could produce 5Y and no X. If resources were concentrated on military activity, the movement would produce 10X and no Y. Between these extremes would be a range of possibilities that might produce a curve such as curve A or curve B in figure 6.

   3. Other significant input factors derive their value from their contribution to one or more of the basic inputs.

A curve of this kind would indicate to the insurgent leader the circumstances under which outputs of one kind could be substituted for outputs of another kind. Looking at points J,

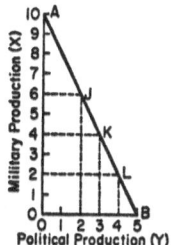

Fig. 6.

K, and L on curve A, B, an insurgent leader could see that the following output mixes would be available to him:

Point J—7X and 2Y
Point K—5X and 3Y
Point L—2X and 4Y

In practice, an insurgent leader might not be able to construct a curve with the precision indicated above, but he would have to make calculations of the kind described here and make decisions based upon those calculations.[4]

Each type of output can be treated as a variable, and there is no one output mix that is always right for every insurgency. In the same way, each input must be regarded as a variable, and the mix of inputs in an insurgency is capable of wide variation. Minimum levels of all the basic inputs are required for the insurgency by definition, but beyond these minimums there is no innput mix that is always right.

The nature of the input mix to be sought will be heavily influenced by the composition of the desired output mix. If political leaders decide to place a heavy emphasis upon political action rather than military action, then the logistics units,

---

4. This analysis is based on the assumption that an insurgent leader will want to make maximum use of available resources at all times. He might, of course, choose to withhold some resources from present use in order to have them available at a later date. In this case he would have to assess the value of present yields against possible future yields.

for example, will have to provide mimeograph machines rather than machine guns, and the training units will have to deal more with the arts of persuasion than the arts of ambush. Whenever a shift in the strategy of an insurgent movement entails changes in the output mix, there are likely to be shifts in the composition of the input mix as well.

How much of a particular input factor will be needed for a given output mix? The answer depends not only on the desired output mix but on the level of production sought. If the movement is operating at a very low level of output, the amounts of each input needed will be modest. In addition, the amount of a needed input will depend on the relationship between that factor and each of the other factors. For example, if an insurgent movement has an unusually good intelligence capability, it will need less of the other factors to achieve a given output level.

Just as outputs are, to some extent, substitutable for one another, basic inputs are also substitutable one for another. This point can be illustrated if attention is focused on any two of the basic inputs, manpower and intelligence for example. The substitutability curve in the figure below indicates the possible mixes of X and Y required for a given result.

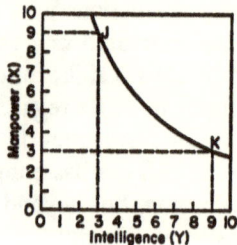

Fig. 7.

For example, if nine units of X are available, only three units of Y will be needed. If only three units of X are available, nine units of Y will be needed.

An insurgent leader in the field may not analyze his problems by using input substitutability curves, but he will nevertheless have to make judgments that could be facilitated by such a curve. He may ask several questions. "If my supplies of weapons are going to be cut, can I compensate for it by an improvement in the intelligence function?" "If the movement has suffered heavy losses among unit commanders, can this loss of leadership be compensated for by improved organizational arrangements?" He will be aware that inputs can be combined in many ways to achieve a given level of output and a given output mix. He will try to take advantage of the fact of substitutability by replacing units of one input with units of another. Without using curves he will probably understand intuitively that a decline in one input factor must be offset by increases in one or more other factors if total output is not to decline.

The leader is also likely to perceive that if he can increase any input factor, without an offsetting decline in other factors, total output will probably increase. Additional increments of that input will not increase output indefinitely, however. If an insurgent movement is inefficiently organized, for example, reorganization will yield high returns, but subsequent reorganizations would yield progressively smaller returns.

Under some circumstances additional increments of an input might even be counterproductive and lead to a decline in the total effectiveness of the movement. It is conceivable that arms might become so plentiful that they would get in the way or that a training program could become so elaborate that it might draw forces away from combat. It is conceivable that a young insurgent movement might acquire more recruits than it could feed, supply, train, and use and that additional increments of manpower might therefore affect the strength of the movement adversely.

Each input factor is susceptible to the principle of decreasing marginal returns. That is, if all other factors are held constant and one factor is increased, at some point the addition of extra units of input will begin to produce progressively smaller numbers of output units. If all the inputs were increased in concert and the proportions among them were maintained, however, there might not need to be a decline in output. There might even be increasing returns to scale; if all the inputs were doubled, the output might be more than doubled. Insurgent movements have not yet been studied sufficiently, however, for this phenomenon to be demonstrated.

This discussion of marginal productivity has assumed that each basic input can be varied. Time has an effect on this variability. In the short run none of these factors can be changed very much. In the long run each can be varied quite substantially. Manpower can be increased by a recruitment program, and intelligence can be improved by better training and better analysis of available information. Leadership can be improved by better training and recruitment. Supply can be improved by the opening of new sources and the development of better means of distribution.

Instead of making a sharp distinction between the short run and the long run and noting the sharply different results that may obtain in each time span, it may be more helpful to think of the variability of most input factors as being curvilinear. In the immediate instant, none of the input factors are variable. As the time span lengthens, however, the capacity of an insurgency to modify an input factor increases, producing a curve similar to that in figure 8. The curve would vary, of course, for each input.

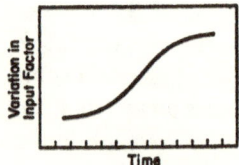

Fig. 8.

There are many proportions in which inputs can be combined in an insurgent movement. Since the basic inputs will be scarce, it is important for the leader to try to combine them in the most efficient way, that is, to achieve a maximum yield at minimum cost. For a given level of output and a given output mix there will be, at any given moment, a minimum-cost combination of inputs. Finding this combination will be difficult, for the ideas of the leaders concerning the proper level of output and output mix will be subject to change as will the relative costs of the basic inputs.

The cost of an input will depend on the energies and resources that have to be expended to acquire it. Scarcity, then, is a basic determinant of cost. If a given input is scarce relative to the other inputs and relative to the demand for it, its cost will be high. If an input is plentiful, its cost will be low. As an insurgent movement consumes an input, its consumption may help make that input scarce. Therefore, an input that was relatively plentiful when the insurgent movement was small may become scarce as the movement expands. High quality leadership is sometimes in short supply in an insurgent movement and may become a more critical factor with the movement's growth. If the supply of weapons to an insurgent movement were fixed for some reason, an increase in the size of the movement would make that factor increasingly important.

Since the cost of each basic input varies over time, the insurgent leader must make periodic adjustments in the composition of the input mix. As input A becomes more scarce and costly, he should design an input mix that relies less on A and more on B and C. Input A should be used sparingly, for high return uses only, and for those uses in which B and C are not adequate substitutes. If input A becomes more plentiful, on the other hand, the movement should utilize more of it and less of B and C. If an insurgent leader could find the point at which the marginal productivity of each input was equal to the marginal productivity of each other input, he would have the minimum-cost input mix.

CHAPTER V
THE CONTEXT OF INSURGENCY

▄▄▄▄ The setting in which an insurgency occurs is likely to have a great impact upon its nature and its outcome. It is helpful to think of this setting in terms of four situational factors: (1) the physical and demographic environment; (2) the strength of the counterinsurgent and the nature of his challenge; (3) the role of traditions, expectations, and attitudes; and (4) the impact of the international environment. In addition, the context in which insurgent conflict takes place is shaped by the fact that insurgency may exhibit some of the characteristics of limited war and by problems associated with the termination of insurgent conflict. This chapter will discuss these matters in the order indicated.

PHYSICAL AND DEMOGRAPHIC ENVIRONMENT

The physical and the demographic features of a country affect the nature and the locus of insurgent military activity. Since he is weak by conventional military standards, the insurgent needs access to a base area or sanctuary which is relatively secure from attack by the counterinsurgent. Ideally, such a region would contain rugged, thickly forested mountains or swamps, an adequate water supply, and either land suitable for farming or proximity to an isolated agricultural district. In addition, it should be large, separated from major population centers, and close to the border of a nation sympathetic with the rebels.

The importance of one terrain element, vegetation, can be seen by contrasting the French experience in Algeria with the American experience in Vietnam. Using a few planes, simple electrified barriers, and surveillance devices, the French were able to patrol a large area and to cut off a substantial portion of the supplies to the FLN coming from Tunisia and Morocco.

In Vietnam, the Americans, making extensive use of a variety of sophisticated aircraft and a variety of advanced technical devices, were never able to interdict the movement of supplies along the Ho Chi Minh Trail even though the area involved was far smaller than that in Algeria. Vegetation explains much of the difference. The French were standing watch on an area that was near desert while the Americans were dealing with a densely forested area.

Terrain facilitates the conduct of some operations and militates against others. Military operations should be undertaken in the daytime only when a rugged, relatively inaccessible refuge is available nearby. Since the guerrillas will typically be operating in small groups, they cannot afford prolonged encounters with the superior manpower and firepower of the enemy. Guevara minimizes the danger of encirclement, since the guerrillas can escape individually after nightfall. However, it is imperative that they be able to fade away into a secure area before the counterinsurgent can relocate them the following day. This requirement places a range limitation upon the operations of the insurgents.[1] An urban insurgency, such as that in Cyprus or Warsaw, is less dependent upon surrounding terrain. The mountains of Cyprus did however provide a refuge for the leaders and an area for staging minor harassing operations.

The density of the population and its composition are factors to be considered in the formulation of insurgent strategies. If the population is highly concentrated, the incumbent regime may be able to insulate the populace from a rural-based insurgent movement. This would deny manpower, intelligence, and logistic support to the rebels. If the population is distributed in a fairly uniform way, on the other hand, it will be almost impossible for the counterinsurgent to protect continuously both the populace and vital installations. The insurgent will find it easier to penetrate the population and to extract needed resources from it.

Climate is another ecological factor. The late David Galula has noted that a mild climate is most favorable from the insurgent standpoint since it permits continuous operations

1. Che Guevara, *Guerrilla Warfare* (New York: Random House, 1961), p. 57.

without posing grave problems of equipment maintenance and survival. "Contrary to the general belief, harsh climates favor the counterinsurgent forces, which have, as a rule, better logistical and operational facilities. This will be especially favorable if the counterinsurgent soldier is a native and, therefore, accustomed to the rigors of the climate. The rainy season in Indochina hampered the Vietminh more than it did the French. Winter in Algeria brought FLN activity almost to a standstill."[2] Galula performed a service by puncturing the long-held notion that climatic extremes are always an advantage for the insurgent. In doing so, however, he passed over the diversity of effects that various climatic conditions may have on different opponents. When air support, including both tactical bombing and troop airlifts, is vital to counterinsurgent operations, monsoon rains may be a severe handicap to the counterinsurgent. Cold weather, on the other hand, may create greater difficulties for the insurgent than for the counterinsurgent since the former lives in rude conditions.

NATURE AND STRENGTH OF THE COUNTER INSURGENT CHALLENGE

The broad political objective of an insurgency will usually be to utilize the population and its resources to make the capability balance more favorable. The strategy to be used in achieving this objective will normally vary with the type of insurgency involved. In the case of an invading army, the strategy may call for building popular support on the base of traditional loyalties and inducing the populace not to co-operate with the invader. If the counterinsurgent is a colonial overlord, the strategy may be to arouse nationalistic fervor, to control the populace, and to demonstrate to the imperialist power that attempts to retain the colony will not be worth the cost involved. When an indigenous regime is in power, however, the political strategy is likely to involve attempts to undermine the legitimacy of the government, to foster a sense of frustration and exploitation in target groups, and to persuade the populace that insurgent rule would be both more efficient and more just.

The military capabilities of the counterinsurgent will nor-

2. David Galula, *Counterinsurgency Warfare: Theory and Practice* (New York: Praeger, 1964), p. 37.

mally have a great influence on the strategy and tactics used by the insurgent. The latter will seek to avoid the counterinsurgent's strengths while exploiting his vulnerabilities. For example, if the counterinsurgent can call upon tactical air support, this has implications for the behavior of the insurgent. Concealment must be nearby, and actions must be terminated quickly. The opponent's mobility is also an important factor. Airmobile units, such as those used by the Americans in South Vietnam and the French in Algeria, can rapidly encircle a guerrilla unit. If the counterinsurgents initiate a maneuver early in the day, they may be able to close the ring and annihilate the insurgents before nightfall. If the guerrillas can hold out until darkness, they will attempt to escape individually through the encirclement. As mentioned earlier, counterinsurgent possession of such an air transport capability places a definite range limitation upon insurgent operations, they cannot safely travel further from a secure area than the distance of a night march.

The mobility provided by land transport vehicles must also be taken into account. Whether cross-country motorized transport, such as that accorded by armored personnel carriers (APC's), or road-bound vehicles alone are at the disposal of the counterinsurgents is a key consideration in tactical planning. Counterinsurgent naval forces may have a role to play in the interdiction of supplies and recruits being delivered to the insurgents by sea. If this is the case, their effectiveness is a factor in strategic planning since the level of insurgent operations is a function of the availability of resources.

The capabilities of the counterinsurgent are determined not only by the equipment available, but also by the quantities of all of the basic input factors at his disposal. The level of operations of the conterinsurgent is governed both by the availability of resources and by his willingness to make the maximum use of them. Therefore, the resource level of the counterinsurgent at any given time is an important factor in determining the operational options open to the insurgent.

TRADITIONS, EXPECTATIONS, AND ATTITUDES

A third situational factor involves the distribution of political, social, economic, cultural, and religious attitudes among the population and the intensity with which various attitudes are held. In conventional conflict, the principal task of the psychological warfare arm is to reduce the enemy's effectiveness by demoralizing his troops. Psychological warfare during an insurgent conflict will not ignore enemy troops, but the principal target will be the population of the country. The insurgent will try to elicit supportive or neutral behavior from the populace. Psychological warfare techniques, in conjunction with the exercise of physical control over people, will also help the insurgents to extract needed resources from the populace.

The existence of cleavages and antagonisms within the society—ethnic, religious, social, economic, political—is to the advantage of the insurgent. While the government must attempt to mediate differences and to calm inflamed tempers, the insurgents will try to exacerbate frictions and make use of internal tensions. They will be eager to contrast the lot of the disadvantaged with that of the well-to-do or to argue that the government is systematically persecuting a political, ethnic, or religious minority.[3] The Catholic-Buddhist schism in South Vietnam, for example, played a key role in the downfall of the Diem Government in 1963 and illustrates the disruptive potential of such cleavages.

An important attitudinal factor affecting the insurgent's choice of population utilization strategies is the degree of social mobilization in the target society. Social mobilization refers to "the pressures that cause populations to form political communities—in other words, the changes that cause people of towns, villages, and regions to knit together into new political orders which transcend these areas as their inhabitants realize that their mutual interests extend beyond daily contacts."[4] If only local and regional allegiances are salient for the populace, the introduction of a disorienting influence (such as a foreign invasion) may provide an opportunity for the insurgents to develop a whole new set of social relationships in the strife-torn society. This is precisely what the Chinese Communists did against the Japanese invaders in

---

3. Ibid., pp. 18–25.
4. Chalmers A. Johnson, *Peasant Nationalism and Communist Power: The Emergence of Revolutionary China, 1939–1945* (Stanford, Calif.: Stanford University Press, 1962), p. 22.

World War II and the Yugoslav Partisans did against the Germans, as Chalmers Johnson has demonstrated. The effort to politicize a provincially oriented peasantry is also characteristic (despite the absence of a newly injected disruption from abroad) of the Malayan, Cuban, Algerian, Philippine, Viet Minh and Viet Cong insurgencies. All have taken place in countries where a widespread sense of national identity was lacking.

The attitudes held by the populace with regard to violence will normally influence the strategies and tactics chosen by the insurgents. As J. K. Zawodny has suggested, it makes a difference whether the local people are Quakers or Catholic Poles when it comes to the use of violence against civilians or the provoking of reprisals by the enemy.[5]

THE INTERNATIONAL ENVIRONMENT

A final situational consideration in the formulation of insurgent strategy relates to the international environment. An insurgent movement may be concerned with foreign affairs for a number of reasons. First, the leaders of an insurgency may want a privileged sanctuary, a base area in an adjoining country with which the counterinsurgent is not at war. The insurgencies in Greece and Algeria demonstrate the importance of such a sanctuary. When hard-pressed, the Communist insurgents in Greece were able to withdraw across the border into Yugoslavia. Tito's closing of this border, following his split with Stalin, denied sanctuary to the insurgents, and they were defeated in 1949.

The insurgents may also be interested in the international realm because of their need for weapons and supplies from abroad. As the weaker party in the conflict, the insurgents must strive to improve the relative balance of resources, and this means seeking resources that may be available in the international environment. Few modern insurgencies have come to power without substantial aid from abroad, and many have come to power with it.

Unless the prospects of an insurgent movement are reasonably good, a foreign government may see no reason to provide

5. J. K. Zawodny, "Unconventional Warfare," *The American Scholar* 31 (Summer 1962).

it with aid and jeopardize relations with the incumbent government.[6]

To establish its prospects an insurgent movement may try to achieve a striking victory or take some important symbolic act such as creating a *de facto* government in a liberated area. The insurgents must bear in mind, however, that outside assistance is not always an unmixed blessing. An insurgent movement may find that its acceptance of outside support is being exploited by the incumbent regime to arouse patriotic sentiment against it. The counterinsurgents can argue that the insurgents are tools of a foreign power. A second danger is that the country offering aid may use its assistance to acquire influence over the insurgent movement. The insurgents may cease to be their own masters and may become virtual tools of the outside power. "If the domestic ally has become dwarfed in terms of autonomous capabilities by the preponderance of outside power, the outcome of the internal war-cum-intervention may be the loss of effective sovereignty and the emergence of another puppet or satellite regime."[7]

An insurgent movement may also be interested in diplomatic recognition as well as foreign aid. This may be the recognition of foreign governments or recognition by international organizations. The existence of international organizations and regional organizations may come to have a substantial influence upon the success of insurgencies. They provide a forum in which the insurgent may have an opportunity to argue his case before a world audience, and regional groupings, such as the Arab League and the OAU, may provide an institutional framework through which foreign assistance to insurgents (or counterinsurgents) may be channeled.

The insurgents may wish to impair the image of the incum-

---

6. ". . . unless and until they have established a position of strength in their own country—that is, unless they have embarked upon an internal war that has a good chance of success—few governments outside the range of their immediate 'sponsors' will wish to have dealings with them, or take them very seriously." George Modelski, "The International Relations of Internal War," in James N. Rosenau, *International Aspects of Civil Strife* (Princeton, New Jersey: Princeton University Press, 1964), p. 27.

7. Karl W. Deutsch, "External Involvement in Internal War," in *Internal War*, ed. Harry Eckstein (New York: The Free Press, 1964), p. 110.

bent regime abroad and damage its international relations. They may hope to deny legitimacy to that regime and to acquire it for the insurgency. This might have important implications in terms of diplomatic recognition and cutting off aid to the government in power.

Trying to influence public and governmental opinion abroad, the insurgents must operate within a given climate of international opinion. If the incumbent regime is a colonial power, it will operate at a considerable disadvantage in the contest for world opinion. As George Modelski has noted, "In recent years, near-universal acceptance has been gained for the view that colonialism is a thing of the past, that all colonial territories ought to be granted independence, and that colonial wars are therefore justified."[8] Insurgencies against colonial regimes will receive a sympathetic hearing in many countries and international organizations.[9]

If the incumbent regime is indigenous, the insurgent movement may seek to label it as neocolonial. The incumbent regime may find itself characterized as barbarous, repressive, and exploitative and may be accused of committing atrocities and genocide. It will not be easy for the foreign press to assess the truth of these charges, and some journals, for ideological reasons, may be inclined to accept them at face value.

INSURGENCY AS LIMITED CONFLICT

In the aftermath of the Korean War, military analysts began to understand that nations could engage in war on a limited basis and that this type of conflict was likely to become common in a world that feared nuclear war but had not eliminated violence as a means for settling disputes. In the late 1950's and early 1960's the concept of limited war began to receive attention and to be subjected to systematic analysis.[10] The concept of limited war is closely related to that of insurgency, and therefore much of the analysis that is appli-

8. Modelski, "International Relations of Internal War," p. 32.
9. See Chapter 17 of Douglas Pike, *Viet Cong* (Cambridge, Mass.: M.I.T. Press, 1966).
10. See Morton H. Halperin, *Limited War in the Nuclear Age* (New York: John Wiley and Sons, 1963) and Seymour J. Deitchman, *Limited War and American Defense Policy* (Cambridge, Mass.: M.I.T. Press, 1964).

cable to the former proves also to be applicable to the latter. In the literature on limited war the antagonists are nation-states. The logic of limited conflict, however, is not confined to nation-states at war but can be applied to many kinds of conflict such as political campaigns, parent-child relationships, labor-management disputes, and street fights. Limited war is a special case within the far broader category of limited conflict that may also include certain kinds of insurgency. In the same way that analysts have, until recently, tended to assume that modern warfare is always an all-out activity, so too they have tended to assume that insurgent conflict is always waged at full throttle. This need not be the case.

At the outset, however, it is important to distinguish between civil insurgencies on the one hand and anticolonial insurgencies and those against an invading army on the other. The stakes are different in the two cases, as has been noted on several occasions. Because the stakes tend to be higher in civil insurgency, the conflict is usually fought more nearly at the capacity of the adversaries. The only restraints observed may be those imposed by the capabilities of the contestants, the dictates of politico-military strategy, or cherished cultural traditions. Agreements, tacit or explicit, are likely to be short lived, and the insurgent will be careful not to deny himself advantages that inhere in the special nature of insurgent conflict. The discussion below, therefore, will apply to civil insurgencies less often than to the other two types.

Just as warfare between nations can be carried on at different levels of activity, so can insurgent conflict. Just as international war can be prosecuted under a variety of constraints and rules of the game, so can insurgent warfare. An insurgency may be limited with respect to geography, level of effort, types of targets hit, weapons used, combat techniques used, and objectives pursued. The restraint may be symmetrical or asymmetrical. That is, it may be practiced by one or both of the antagonists. The restraint would be asymmetrical, for example, if a counterinsurgent force were devoting a limited proportion of its energies to combatting an insurgent force that was delivering its utmost effort.

The rhetoric and pretensions of insurgent conflict may make it difficult for either the insurgent or the counterinsurgent to acknowledge that he is practicing restraint. The counterinsurgent wants to assure supporters that the struggle against the criminals, bandits, and traitors who are the enemy is being prosecuted in a whole-hearted way and without letup. A discussion of the degree of vigor that should be used against an insurgent would undermine the image of stern resolution which the counterinsurgent is probably trying to convey. For reasons of morale and ideology, the insurgent usually finds it useful to portray the counterinsurgent as a ruthless oppressor of the people. Having done so, it is then difficult to justify anything short of an all-out, unrelenting struggle.

It is often helpful to distinguish between the formal, announced goals of an insurgent movement and the operational goals revealed by the behavior of the leaders and of the movement. As suggested above, the rhetorical objective of the movement may be to attack the enemy in an unrelenting way while the operational objective may be more modest. Another reason the formal goals and the operational goals may be different is that the leaders of an insurgency may have a set of secondary, unannounced goals that modify the movement's official goals.

A discussion of limited insurgent conflict raises a number of interesting questions. When will a contestant want to escalate a conflict and when will he want to de-escalate it?[11] What keeps a limited insurgent conflict limited? Under what circumstances would such a limitation prove unstable? When might the insurgent and the counterinsurgent have a common interest in co-ordinating their behavior to a degree?[12] Each side might conclude that its interest would not be advanced by escalation and might therefore want to avoid it. The insurgent and the counterinsurgent need not necessarily have the same reason for pursuing a restrained policy. The insurgent might be playing for time or awaiting some favorable political development while the counterinsurgent might believe that the existing level of conflict would soon exhaust the enemy.

The contestants may also have a common interest in devel-

---

11. Matters relating to escalation and deescalation are discussed in Chapter III.
12. The extent of such common interest is likely to be much reduced in the case of a civil insurgency.

oping certain rules to govern the conduct of the conflict. It might serve the interest of both sides if it were mutually understood that no one is to use torture, that there are to be no attempts at assassinating the leaders of the other side, that fighting will cease during religious holidays, and that there is to be a moratorium on serious conflict during the winter months.

If the antagonists have a common interest in agreeing on a level at which the conflict shall be prosecuted and on certain rules of the game, how are they to achieve this co-ordination under circumstances in which communication is severely limited. Thomas C. Schelling has posed the issue: "The problem is to develop a modus vivendi when one or both parties either cannot or will not negotiate explicitly or when neither would trust the other with respect to any agreement explicitly reached."[13] His answer to the problem is, of course, that enemies can engage in tacit bargaining. "The study of tacit bargaining—bargaining in which communication is incomplete or impossible—assumes importance, therefore, in connection with limited war, or, for that matter, with limited competition, jurisdictional maneuvers, jockeying in a traffic jam, or getting along with a neighbor that one does not speak to."[14] Agreement can emerge in a conflict situation without explicit negotiation. That holds true for insurgent conflict as well as for conflict between warring nations. Both the insurgent and the counterinsurgent might become aware of the element of restraint in a particular situation, and each might want to preserve that restraint. In such a situation a tacit bargain can be struck if each combatant exhibits restraint. By his restraint, each is saying to the other, "I do not plan to do anything untoward, and will not, unless you force me to." Seasonal lulls in insurgent conflict and reductions in activity during religious holidays have sometimes emerged from tacit bargains. Tacit agreements have sometimes emerged, and remained stable for a time, concerning the geographical limits of the struggle. The counterinsurgent may refrain from going into the hills after the insurgent, and the insurgent in turn

---

13. Thomas C. Schelling, *The Strategy of Conflict* (Cambridge, Mass.: Harvard University Press, 1960), p. 53.
14. Ibid.

may refrain from attacking towns or army barracks and embarrassing the counterinsurgent.[15] In this way the hills may belong to the insurgent and the towns to the counterinsurgent, and the struggle between the antagonists will revolve around the road system and the attempt to move personnel and supplies.

A tacit rule may emerge, may be observed for a time, and then may begin to be ignored by one or both antagonists. It is in the nature of a tacit rule that it will usually be observed only as long as each side believes it to be in its interest to observe it. To be sure, one side might continue to observe a particular rule even though it was disadvantageous to do so in order not to endanger the observance by the other wise of the entire structure of rules that might exist. On the whole, however, the stability of a rule is governed by the immediate interests and capabilities of the antagonists. A tacit rule is a special kind of rule. Since it is unwritten and has not been formally agreed to, the antagonists will feel no pressure to adhere to it because of the general principle that rules must be obeyed. It is not that kind of rule. If the insurgent perceives that the counterinsurgent has been so weakened politically and militarily that he cannot respond to an escalation of the conflict with a sharp counterescalation, the insurgent would feel free to ignore the tacit agreement that has stabilized the level of effort and to increase the pressure against the counterinsurgent.

TERMINATION OF INSURGENT CONFLICT

This volume has discussed the origins of insurgency and its dynamics, but little has been said about how insurgent conflict might be ended. Such conflict can be terminated either through negotiated settlement or through victory for one side and defeat for the other. There are variations of each of these types, of course. For example, an insurgent movement may dissolve without suffering a decisive defeat and without surrendering formally.

A negotiated settlement requires dialogue between the leaders of the opposing sides. The dialogue can be carried on

---

15. An agreement of this kind will be unusual in a civil insurgency.

face to face, in writing, or through intermediaries. It can also be carried on in the press by means of a series of unilateral announcements, ultimatums, and responses. This last method would allow the leaders to negotiate without making an explicit acknowledgement that they were negotiating. Indeed, in the early stages of feeling out one another, they might not be fully aware that they were, in fact, negotiating.

The course of the negotiations, when started, will be influenced by the communications process involved and by several other factors. It will be influenced by the objectives of each side. Leaders may have to learn to distinguish between the objectives they proclaim in their rhetoric and the gains they would actually be willing to settle for. The negotiations will also be influenced by the normal drift of objectives. The initial objectives of an insurgent movement may be modest and reformist in nature, but these may gradually be replaced by more ambitious goals as the struggle continues and as the criticism of the counterinsurgent becomes more throughgoing and the struggle generates increased bitterness. The negotiations will also be influenced by the success, or lack of success, that each side is enjoying in the field. Success in the field will normally lead to an expansion of goals and a hardening of a bargaining position while reverses will lead to the reverse. In addition, the negotiations will be influenced by the stakes involved and by the way each side conceives its future prospects.

Initially each side will be loathe to consider a negotiated settlement. Formal negotation is likely to be incompatible with the rhetoric that each engages in and with its statement of objectives. Prolonged conflict and stalemate, however, may lead the antagonists to be more receptive to the idea of a negotiated settlement. This would be particularly the case if the insurgent leaders had important secondary objectives that might be jeopardized by prolonged fighting. Each side may begin to sense that it will have to settle for something less than the total surrender of the enemy and the complete achievement of its own objectives. The counterinsurgent may begin to wonder whether the costs of continuing the struggle might not outweigh those of instituting some of the reforms demanded by the insurgent. The insurgent, in turn, might be willing to give up some of his more extreme demands in return for concessions on other points and a promise of amnesty.

Since the stakes are normally higher in civil insurgencies than in other insurgencies, termination of the conflict may present special problems. The interests of the adversaries are more likely to be defined in zero-sum terms, and there will be less room for negotiation and bargaining. In any settlement, the terms finally agreed upon will be the result of a bargaining process. Bargaining does not necessarily cease simply because the two parties are at war with one another.

War is always a bargaining process, one in which threats and proposals, counterproposals and counterthreats, offers and assurances, concessions and demonstrations, take the form of actions rather than words, or actions accompanied by words. It is in the wars that we have come to call "limited wars" that the bargaining appears most vividly and is conducted most consciously. The critical targets in such a war are in the mind of the enemy as much as on the battlefield; the state of the enemy's expectations is as important as the state of his troops; the threat of violence in reserve is more important than the commitment of force in the field.[16]

Even if one side were slowly defeating the other, a bargaining relationship might still exist. The negotiation would then be over the terms of the surrender. If the counterinsurgents believed that they were winning, their spokesmen might say to the insurgents, "You are going to be defeated sooner or later. The longer you resist the greater will be the damage inflicted upon you. Since it is costly for us to have to continue inflicting this damage, it is in the interest of *both* of us that you should surrender, and the sooner the better." The insurgent might respond to this line of argument by asking what concessions the counterinsurgent was prepared to make to obtain this surrender. Despite the fact that the insurgent might have some bargaining power even in defeat, his position would, of course, be clearly the weaker of the two. An aroused antagonist might choose to make no concessions whatever except amnesty for those who deserted the insurgents or surrendered.

This discussion has assumed that both antagonists are capa-

---

16. Thomas C. Schelling, *Arms and Influence* (New Haven: Yale University Press, 1966), pp. 142–43.

ble of rational analysis of their own interests and can examine as sensitive a topic as surrender with a degree of detachment. In some cases, such as a bitter civil insurgency or a prolonged and bitter anticolonial insurgency, this assumption may not be valid. The insurgent, even if he is losing, may pledge to fight to the end despite the readiness of the counterinsurgent to negotiate. The counterinsurgent, in winning, may be implacable. Instead of promising amnesty he may demand unconditional surrender and look forward to the moment when the last of the insurgents are in his power and helpless. If the insurgent had been almost ready to discuss surrender, the demand for unconditional surrender might strengthen his will to resist and prolong the struggle.

All insurgent movements proclaim a common goal—victory. The operational meaning of victory is subject to great variation, however. Victory may mean one thing to one set of leaders and something quite different to another set. One set, while proclaiming victory as its objective, may be prepared to settle for less than the other set. Unless the concept of victory is given a more specific content by the use of mediating concepts, it may actually mislead the insurgent or the counterinsurgents. Success in insurgent conflict should not be defined in narrowly military terms. As the term is normally used, victory for one antagonist is presumed to imply the defeat of the other. In a military struggle, this suggests that victory can be won only if the enemy is defeated militarily. In an insurgent conflict, however, the struggle may be won without a victory that is signaled by the military defeat of the enemy, and a decisive military engagement may not result in the termination of the conflict.

Insurgent victory, for example, may not hinge on the military defeat of the enemy but upon the enemy's analysis of the cost of prolonging the struggle. In the case of Algeria and again in the case of Cyprus the struggle went on and on, and the costs—casualties, material losses, domestic political costs, diplomatic costs, costs in world opinion, cost of having troops tied down and unavailable for other uses—continued to mount. As the cumulative costs of the struggle became greater the counterinsurgent leaders began to wonder if those costs did not outweigh any benefits that could reasonably be expected from continuing the struggle. Finally, they concluded that the costs were unacceptable and, at the conference table, agreed to relinquish that which the insurgents had never been able to wrest from them in the field.

The insurgent will probably not be able to locate with accuracy the point at which the costs of prolonging the struggle will be deemed unacceptable by the counterinsurgents. Its location will vary with the type of insurgency involved and with the stage of a given insurgency. In an age of anticolonialism, colonial regimes have sometimes proved easily discouraged. In the case of a domestic insurgency, the counterinsurgent leaders are probably prepared to fight to the bitter end since defeat means death or exile. By raising the costs of the conflict, however, the insurgents may be able to set forces in motion which may lead to the overthrow of the incumbent regime.

In his propaganda the insurgent may want to emphasize the pursuit of victory, but in his planning he will be better advised to focus upon the objective of raising the costs of the struggle to the enemy. The concept of victory, by itself, has little operational significance, but the cost concept is easy to understand and may provide a day-by-day guide that shows the way to ultimate success for the movement. Insurgent leaders, both in headquarters and in field units, can examine proposed alternative courses of action in terms of the relative costs of each to the counterinsurgent and the insurgent.

The existence of emotional fervor or strong hatred can alter the cost picture because of the impact it has on the morale and determination of the antagonists. The insurgent will to resist may be nourished by hatred of a social class and attendant exploitation or by a passionate nationalist hatred of a foreign oppressor. The counterinsurgent may lack such energizing motivation. In the case of the Algerian insurgency, for example, the French were a long way from home and knew they were not fighting for the survival of France. In view of this motivational asymmetry, it is not surprising that the French finally succumbed to exhaustion and despair. The costs of the struggle continued to mount, and neither the interests of France nor the motivation of the French forces dictated its prolongation.

Stated generally, the problem facing the counterinsurgent is how to subdue an enemy that hates him implacably. A central objective in most warfare is the destruction of the enemy's will to resist. This is normally accomplished by inflicting military defeats upon the enemy in the field. What is one to do, however, if defeat does not weaken his will but leaves it unchanged or even strengthens it? If emotional fervor is great enough, a defeat may not be accepted as a defeat. An insurgent unit may be defeated and dispersed, but, instead of surrendering, the survivors disappear into the hills and vow revenge. Despite heavy losses the leaders of the movement may vow to fight until the counterinsurgents are dead or driven from the land. Eventually the counterinsurgent must begin to wonder how important his military victories are and how he is to terminate the conflict. In the case of the Algerian, Cypriot, Palestinian, and Tunisian insurgencies, the insurgents did not win their wars in the traditional military sense, and the counterinsurgents were not defeated; they simply despaired of ever winning. They despaired of ever being able to govern on the basis of willing co-operation from the local residents.

If the insurgent refuses to surrender despite defeats, this reduces the options open to the counterinsurgent for terminating the conflict. A negotiated settlement is eliminated, and he may have to consider waging a virtual war of extermination. The physical cost and, more importantly, the political cost of waging such a war may be prohibitive. If that is the case, the counterinsurgent may then have to consider giving up the fight himself. If one cannot defeat an enemy, one may ultimately be defeated.

CHAPTER VI

INSURGENT STRATEGY AND TACTICS

━━━ This chapter is divided into two parts. The first section will examine strategic considerations and objectives relevant to an insurgency. Section two will focus upon tactical objectives and the techniques used to achieve them. A comparative perspective is helpful in the study of insurgency, and this chapter will be written from such a perspective. Individuals analyzing insurgency commonly make the mistake of basing their generalizations primarily upon the lessons of their own experience. This leads to the peculiar being mistaken for the universal. Writers assume that the features of an insurgency with which they have become familiar are common to all insurgencies. In fact, behavior that is appropriate to one insurgency may not be appropriate to another and may not be found there.

This chapter will also stress the interplay of political and military action that characterizes insurgencies. It is the combination of political action and guerrilla tactics that differentiates insurgency from rural banditry on the one hand and conventional warfare on the other. Writers on insurgency have mistakenly tended to emphasize the military aspect and neglect the political. Even so experienced a theoretician and practitioner as Che Guevara could define guerrilla strategy without reference to the over-all political objectives of the Cuban revolution.[1]

Because of the interplay of political and military factors in an insurgency, efforts to make a sharp distinction between the two are usually not very helpful. A distinction cannot be made on the basis of personnel (military or political) because an insurgent is often both a military and a political figure. The

1. Che Guevara, *Guerrilla Warfare* (New York: Random House, 1961), p. 8.

nature of the technique used does not provide the basis for distinguishing the two because some techniques, such as the use of terror, are both military and political. The nature of the target of the action does not provide a clear basis for distinction, nor does the nature of the objective, nor does the nature of the consequences that result from the action. An insurgent detachment may ambush an insurgent squad. The action has an obvious military result (counterinsurgent casualties, loss of supplies), but it may also have a political result. It may persuade the local villagers that the insurgents are going to win the struggle. In short, personnel that are military or political (or both) can use techniques that are military or political (or both) against targets that are military or political (or both) in the pursuit of objectives that are military or political (or both) and produce consequences that are military or political (or both). The diagram below may be helpful in illustrating the point.

The capabilities of an insurgent movement have a compelling influence upon strategy and tactics. They establish the broad parameters within which the movement can operate at any given time. Indeed, the reason guerrilla warfare was utilized in the first instance may have been because the movement lacked the means to carry on the struggle in a more direct and orthodox manner.[2] At the beginning of the conflict the discrepancy in relative capabilities is likely to be great, and this will severely restrict the options open to the insurgent. A basic element in the long-run strategy of the insurgent must be to try to increase the level of his capabilities as the conflict progresses and reduce those of his opponent. As noted earlier, the insurgent improves his capabilities by increasing

---

2. This may not be the case, of course, if the insurgency has been fomented by a foreign power. That power may have the means to attack the government of the target country by orthodox means but may choose not to for any of a variety of reasons.

the basic inputs—leadership and organization, intelligence, manpower, logistic support, and population utilization.

The factor limiting the scope of insurgent activities at a given moment, however, is not merely the matter of the relative capabilities of the two movements. Risk must figure in every calculation, for as a rule the insurgent leader cannot afford losses. This means that he must usually avoid combat when the odds are only moderately favorable and wait until they are overwhelmingly in his favor. Paradoxically, although guerrilla operations may appear bold and daring from a distance, the preoccupation with minimizing combat risks often introduces a distinctly conservative bias. Over and over again an insurgent leader will decline to accept combat when facing odds that the commander of a regular unit in the armed forces would regard as quite acceptable. In Guevara's words, "The fundamental principle is that no battle, combat, or skirmish is to be fought unless it will be won."[3] Mao Tse-tung's counsel was, "Retreat when attacked."

As the capabilities of the insurgent movement increase, the insurgent leader is subjected to a special form of temptation, that of trying to beat the enemy at his own game. General Giap succumbed to this temptation during his premature excursion into conventional warfare in the Red River Delta during the spring of 1951.[4] Col. J. C. Murray has described the consequences for the Greek Communists following their decision to operate in larger units and to commit themselves to the defense of the Vitsi-Grammos area:

> The tendency of the Democratic Army during 1948 and 1949 toward a military strategy that depended for its success upon the organization of larger formations and the employment of orthodox military tactics implied a growing reliance upon military force alone. Under the existing conditions, any such development played into the hands of the government forces. . . . The decisive defeat of the guerrillas was made possible by their departure from proper guerrilla organization and tactics in their effort to defend the base areas along the frontier and the gathering of their one-time small bands into larger formations ranging in size up to the division.[5]

3. Guevara, *Guerrilla Warfare*, p. 6.
4. Bernard B. Fall, *The Two Viet-Nams* (New York: Praeger, 1967), pp. 114–17.
5. Col. J. C. Murray, "The Anti-Bandit War," in Lt. Col. T. N. Greene, ed., *The Guerrilla—and How to Fight Him* (New York: Praeger, 1962), p. 111.

When the insurgent abandons guerrilla tactics and seeks to fight on the enemy's terms, he discards the peculiar advantages that the insurgent mode of conflict confers upon him. This does not mean that the insurgent should never engage in conventional operations, but it does mean that this step should be undertaken only after the most careful examination.

In the political realm, in contrast to the military realm, the level of insurgent operations is likely to be much closer to the movement's actual capabilities. Here, also, the movement must be concerned with increasing its capabilities and reducing those of the counterinsurgent. In liberated areas the insurgents must try to solidify their hold upon the populace. Attempting to do this, many avenues are open to them, from coercion at one extreme to enlightened reform and persuasion at the other. In contested areas the political options open to the insurgents will depend upon the activities of the counterinsurgents as well as upon the objectives of the insurgents and their local capabilities.

STRATEGIC OBJECTIVES AND TACTICAL CONSIDERATIONS

A central factor in the determination of insurgent objectives is the identity of the opponent. The stakes for an indigenous regime, a colonial power, and a foreign invader are obviously different, as are the means of response each may deem appropriate. The very lives of a native elite may hang in the balance, while the loss of a colony is a somewhat lesser calamity for a colonial administration, and an alien conqueror may base his response to the insurgent upon the military value of the country alone. Such considerations will substantially influence the insurgent's choice of objectives, targets, and techniques.

The stated objectives of a movement will have an impact upon the populace and will largely determined which elements of the population can be looked to for support and which for opposition. If the objectives of the movement can be stated in such a way as to appeal to both patriotism and discontent, the movement may have a bright future. An insurgent leader will usually have a degree of freedom of action in the way in which he enunciates the objectives of the movement, but once the objectives have been enunciated they will serve to constrain the movement to some extent thereafter. If reforms have been promised, for example, the failure to institute such measures in liberated areas would raise doubts about the sincerity of the leaders of the movement.

The aim of an insurgent movement is to accomplish the goals it has set, and these may be varied. It can accomplish its goals, however, only if it survives. Therefore, while the survival of the movement is not in itself the ultimate objective, it is indispensable to the achievement of that objective, and therefore it is a central consideration in insurgent decision making.

The over-all *strategic* objective of the insurgents is to alter the relative capabilities balance in their favor, and this can be done by modifying the input flows for each side. It is helpful to distinguish also three subordinate strategic objectives: 1) improved population utilization; 2) an improved military situation; and 3) successful influencing of the international environment. Trying to achieve these objectives, the insurgents will focus upon four main targets: (1) the indigenous population; (2) the civil administration; (3) the counterinsurgent's

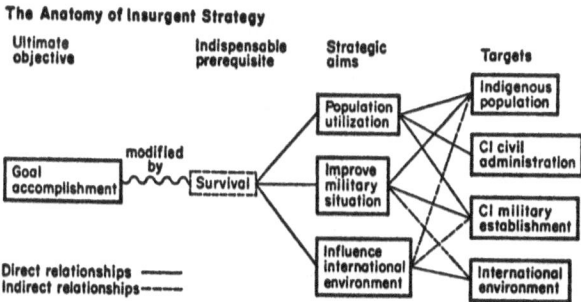

Fig. 1.

military establishment; and (4) the international environment. Figure 1 indicates graphically the way in which goal accomplishment, survival, strategic objectives, and targets are related one to another. This figure also shows that activities focused upon one target may have an impact upon other targets as well.

To achieve these strategic objectives and strike against the four strategic targets, the insurgent will define for himself a second layer of objectives, targets, and supporting activities.

94 ▪ INSURGENCY

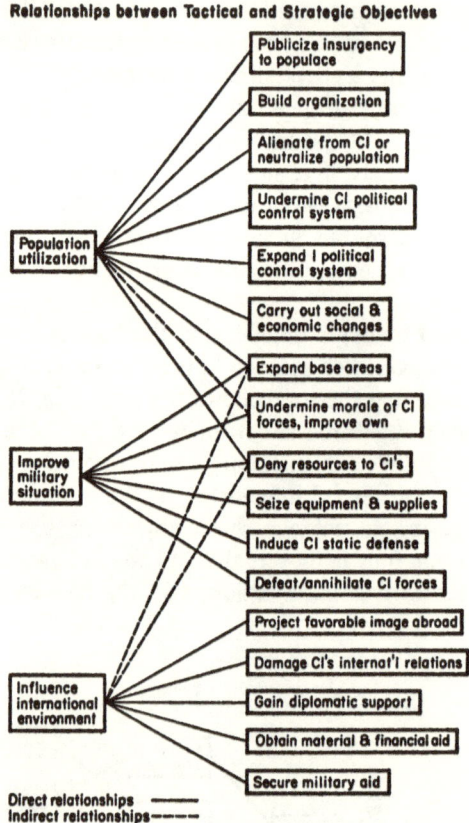

Fig. 2.

For purposes of convenience, these may be referred to as tactical objectives, targets, and activities.[6] The relationship between the strategic objectives and tactical objectives and activities is indicated in figure 2. Here again it is clear that tactical objectives and activities may contribute simultaneously, directly or indirectly, to the achievement of more than one strategic objective.

6. The distinction between strategy and tactics is a formal one and forces the analyst to make a set of arbitrary distinctions. In practice there is no natural breaking point but only a series of gradations from objectives and activities that are of the highest generality at one extreme to those that are specific at the other. When the situation involves a continuum the use of dichotomous terminology can sometimes be confusing and impede insight.

In the pages that follow each of the three strategic objectives will be discussed in connection with the tactical objectives and activities most closely related to them.

POPULATION UTILIZATION

The population, and its associated resources, may be viewed as an instrument to be used by the insurgents in their struggle against the counterinsurgents. It is in the interest of the insurgents to utilize the population as efficiently as possible. As explained earlier, population utilization is not the same thing as popular support. Mao Tse-tung's writings and the example of the Chinese Communist revolt have impressed upon many insurgent leaders, particularly other Communists, the importance of popular support as a key to victory.[7] However, the population may contribute quite handsomely to the insurgent movement without ever making an ideological commitment. Behavior, not attitudes, is the crucial factor. The proper measure of the success of the insurgent's population utilization efforts is their ability to draw from the populace the desired behavior and needed resources.

The relations between populace and insurgents are subject to wide variation. At one extreme, the insurgents may have the voluntary and enthusiastic cooperation of the populace. At the other, they may have to use coercive measures to neutralize the antagonism of the populace. The relationship between the insurgents and the populace at a given moment can be conceived of as falling somewhere along a continuum, a compliance continuum.

Coercion and Compliance in Insurgent-Mass Relations

Maximum Force		Minimum Force
Neutralization	Forced Cooperation	Institutionalized, Voluntary Cooperation

The insurgents will strive to move the relationship as far to the right along this continuum as possible, consistent with

7. Peter Paret and John W. Shy point out the centrality of popular support in Communist thinking on revolution in *Guerrillas in the 1960's*, Rev. ed. (New York: Praeger, 1966), pp. 18–21.

other objectives. If they have some success in this respect, the population will produce voluntarily, upon demand, the supplies, recruits, and information desired. Insurgent efforts at population utilization can be discussed under two broad rubrics, undermining the enemy's population utilization system and establishing the insurgent's population utilization system.

Undermining the Enemy's Population Utilization System
The greater the insurgent control over an area, the greater the percentage of that area's resources the insurgent can normally utilize. The same holds for the counterinsurgents. This means that if the insurgents wish to increase the percentage of an area's resources available to the movement they must reduce counterinsurgent control over that area. Setting aside possible changes in the total amount of resources that can be generated in a given area, it appears that insurgents and counterinsurgents are involved in a zero-sum game.

If the insurgents want to utilize the population in an area over which they do not have effective control, they must first pry loose the populace from the enemy's population utilization system. There are three nonmilitary elements in the counterinsurgent's population utilization system: (1) the political structure; (2) the police; and (3) the administrative bureaucracy. These elements are used to control the populace and are therefore targets for insurgent activity.

The political structure shapes the relationship between the government and the individual citizen. At one extreme there may be the tight control associated with a modern totalitarian dictatorship and at the other the loose political arrangements often found in a developing country. Tight political control, combined with a pervasive police function, makes it difficult to initiate an insurgent movement or to expand it.

The police act in a dual role as protectors of the local populace against insurgent attacks and pressure and as a key element in the counterinsurgent intelligence network. The police must be weakened before the insurgents can begin to utilize the population to any extent. Threats and violence against the police may achieve the desired result. When the EOKA was active in Cyprus, many Cypriot law officers resigned or looked the other way for reasons of personal safety.

Terror might be used by the insurgent as a means of undermining the counterinsurgent's control system. Terror must be viewed as primarily a political instrument rather than a military instrument. It is used against the enemy's control apparatus or is used to cow the populace, but it is rarely used against counterinsurgent military forces in the hope of inflicting military defeat.

The identity and behavior of the opponent will influence the readiness with which an insurgent resorts to terror. Against an alien invader, who would not hesitate to resort to harsh reprisals, the insurgent might avoid the use of terror. After the German occupation of Yugoslavia, disagreement over the wisdom of insurgent use of terror tactics was one of the factors that widened the rift between Tito and Mikhailovitch.[8]

An indigenous regime would normally hesitate to take reprisals against the populace because of the hatred that such actions would produce. Knowing that, insurgent leaders might feel free to use terror against the incumbents. They would not need to fear that the government would establish harsh control measures and that the people would charge the insurgents with having provoked those actions.

The government's position is a difficult one when subjected to terrorist attacks. The insurgent movement has no trouble identifying representatives of the government and striking at them. The government is not able to identify individual insurgents, and therefore, if it wants to combat acts of terrorism, it has no alternative but to institute control measures that affect the entire population—curfews, travel papers, identity cards, searches. Its dilemma is that it must either suffer the terrorism without taking action or must take action and suffer the consequences of doing so.

Under some circumstances the insurgents might try to draw the government into taking reprisals against the people in the hope that such actions would speed the government's downfall. Terror is not a normal feature of political conflict in Latin America, and it has been claimed that "Batista's desperate

---

8. Otto Heilbrunn, *Partisan Warfare* (New York: Praeger, 1962), p. 22.

resort to terror in his last year probably contributed more than Castro's charismatic qualities to his final downfall."[9]

The use of terror is dangerous for the user as well as for those against whom it is used. In Malaya the MRLA engaged in indiscriminate terror for a time—shooting up buses, throwing grenades in cinemas. Before long it was realized that these attacks were proving to be counterproductive.[10] In South Vietnam the Viet Cong instituted a terror campaign against members of the bureaucratic structure. Assassinations of local leaders, such as village chiefs and teachers, reached the proportions of an extermination campaign. It is hard to evaluate the long-term result of the campaign, but it is perhaps significant that the campaign was subsequently cut back sharply. In addition to striking directly at the counterinsurgent control apparatus themselves, the insurgents may be able to use the populace against that control apparatus. They might organize strikes, popular demonstrations, and riots to embarrass and weaken the government or force it into excesses.

Establishing the Insurgent Population Utilization Apparatus
An insurgency cannot begin to use the resources of a population effectively until the existence of the insurgency is known to the people. One of the first tasks of the insurgent movement, therefore, will be to spread the word. Perhaps the most effective announcement of an insurgency's inception was the Algerian FLN's co-ordinated, nationwide wave of spectacular acts of indiscriminate terrorism on the last day of October, 1954. French censorship was unable to prevent discussion of these events, so the movement was able to gain wide publicity and signal its arrival on the scene by a single stroke.

Dramatic effect should be weighed against other considerations however. Indiscriminate terror of the kind referred to

---

9. Carl Leiden and Karl M. Schmitt, *The Politics of Violence: Revolution in the Modern World* (Englewood Cliffs, N. J.: Prentice-Hall, Inc., 1968), p. 34.
10. Sir Robert Thompson, *Defeating Communist Insurgency: The Lessons of Malaya and Vietnam* (New York: Praeger, 1966), p. 25. See also Lucien W. Pyle, *Guerrilla Communism in Malaya* (Princeton, N. J.: Princeton University Press, 1956), pp. 95–111 for a more thorough discussion of the reasons the MCP chose terrorism and the constraints this decision placed on future activities.

above could give an unfortunate first impression of the movement and antagonize the very people it was designed to influence. Furthermore, acts of terrorism signified the existence of the movement not only to the Algerians but to the French government as well and might have prematurely endangered the movement.

Once strong roots have been established in a base area, selective terrorism may be employed to help expand popular awareness of the insurgency. The target of the terrorism would be individuals associated with the counterinsurgent's population control apparatus. In addition, the insurgents may seek journalistic attention, circulate literature, hold open meetings where it is safe, and do other things to gain attention.

The success of the insurgent's domestic publicity efforts will be influenced by the cause they are trying to sell to the populace and by the response of the populace to the cause. How important the cause is in winning popular support (as distinct from its importance to the morale of the insurgent troops) is not altogether clear, however. Some writers have taken its importance for granted while other writers have deemed it of peripheral significance. T. E. Lawrence's claim that an insurgency could be successful with the active support of two percent of the population and the apathetic resignation of the remainder suggests that the cause is not invariably significant.

A great deal depends on the type of insurgency involved. If it is an insurgency against a foreign invader, the cause will probably generate widespread patriotic feelings the insurgent can then translate into supportive behavior. If the insurgency is against a colonial power, the cause of casting off foreign domination may well become a focal point for nascent nationalism.[11]

In the case of civil insurgencies, the effectiveness of the cause varies with circumstances. On the whole, however, its effectiveness appears limited. It appears to be more difficult to

---

11. Even here, however, the picture is sometimes clouded. In the case of the Angolan insurgency, for example, "few, if any, of the African villagers show any inclination to side with the rebels." "Africa's Unreported War," *U. S. News and World Report* (June 10, 1968), p. 69.

get support for violence against one's fellow countrymen than against foreigners. When the enemy is the foreigner, the situation is unambiguous. In the case of a civil insurgency, however, individual citizens may feel that the situation is ambiguous and uncertain and may therefore be inclined to withhold their loyalty.

When an abstract cause proves ineffective in eliciting the desired behavior from the populace, the insurgents may seek to gain support on the basis of various local issues. "The indifference of the villager [in South Vietnam] to the abstract cause of reunification forced the NLF to concentrate on local complaints as a means of winning village support, for local grievances and proposals to end them could be understood and evaluated by any villager. When legitimate grievances did exist, and they did under Diem, the villager was inclined to support the NLF."[12] Irrespective of the issue around which an insurgent movement centers, an imaginative leader will usually have little difficulty modifying the cause by adding new elements and subtracting the old. The experienced leader is likely to have an instrumental approach to the movement's ideology or cause.

Given a basic cause, many other issues can be tacked onto it, such as land for the landless, exploitation of labor on estates and mines, regional autonomy for ethnic minorities and political equality for immigrant races with the indigenous races. At the same time, all local seeds of conflict within a community can be exploited. . . . There is always some issue which has an appeal to each section of the community, and, even if dormant, an inspired incident may revive it in an acute form. This particularly applies during the course of the insurgency itself, when new causes can be developed from events, and, if necessary, old ones be forgotten.[13]

Once the insurgents have established effective military control over an area they will be in a position to install the political and administrative apparatus that will allow them to utilize the population and resources in that area. One of their high priority objectives will be the mobilization and political activation of the populace. They may make use of ritual trials. This eliminates a bureaucrat or other enemy, offers a warning

12. Douglas Pike, *Viet Cong* (Cambridge, Mass.: M.I.T. Press, 1966), p. 54.
13. Thompson, *Defeating Communist Insurgency*, pp. 21–22.

to potential enemies or obstructors, and involves the people in a common activity. Douglas Pike has noted that one of the two main objectives of the NLF movement in South Vietnam was "to engage, activate, and immerse the persons involved in the revolution."[14]

The insurgents may also establish a network of organizations to help orient the populace, to regulate their activity, to draw them into supportive activity, and to provide an instrument for surveillance and pressure. In some of the areas in South Vietnam, in which the Viet Cong's control was not seriously challenged for several years, the functional and associational groups organized by the NLF were quite successful in eliciting voluntary co-operation from the populace. Douglas Pike has discussed the significance of these associations.

In the NLF-controlled areas it threw a net of associations over the rural Vietnamese that could seduce him into voluntarily supporting the NLF or, failing that, bring the full weight of social pressure to bear on him, or, if both of these failed, could compel his support. It could subject him effectively to surveillance, indoctrination, and exploitation. It could order his life. It could artificially create grievances and develop support where logically such support ought not to have been forthcoming.

The purpose of this vast organizational effort was not simply population control but to restructure the social order of the village and train the villagers to control themselves. This was the NLF's one undeviating thrust from the start . . . organization in depth of the rural population through the instrument of self-control—victory by means of the organizational weapon.[15]

During the war against Japan and again in the war against the Chinese Nationalists, Mao Tse-tung established organizations that functioned in much the way described above. In the hands of capable insurgent leaders institutionalization can be an effective instrument.

Once the political and administrative apparatus is established, the insurgents will be able to control behavior to a considerable extent and to influence popular attitudes through the use of schools, public meetings, and various forms of printed and oral propaganda. They may wish to levy taxes, to establish conscription, and to expropriate certain kinds of

14. Pike, *Viet Cong*, p. 92.
15. Ibid., p. 111.

property. In short, the insurgents will be in a position to function as a virtual government in the area and to make full and systematic use of whatever resources are available.

When the matter is viewed in this light, the magnitude of the task (and of the opportunity) becomes clearer. If the insurgents seek to establish an elaborate apparatus and an ambitious set of controls, the administrative burden will be great. They may conclude that the advantages of such a program more than offset the disadvantages. It would give the insurgent leaders experience in governing and would ensure a greater flow of resources toward the movement. In addition, in the event that the insurgents were forced to evacuate the area, they would be able to leave behind them a fully developed apparatus for information collection, recruitment, logistical support, terrorism, and a variety of political and agitational activities.

Despite the effectiveness of organizational controls there will probably be some recalcitrant individuals. As the *de facto* government of the area, the insurgents may decide to utilize "enforcement terror."[16] Since the insurgency controls the area and is functioning as a government, such action represents its exercise of the police function.

MILITARY ACTIVITIES

Insurgent military activities are usually not designed to achieve a single objective but a cluster of objectives: expansion of its base area; resource re-allocation; undermining enemy morale; inducing a static defense posture; and increasing the cost to the enemy of continuing the struggle.

Expansion of the Base Area

If an insurgent movement is to advance toward military victory, it must normally augment its capabilities vis-à-vis the enemy. It can do this by reducing the capabilities of the enemy or by expanding its own capabilities. Expansion of the

---

16. Thomas Perry Thornton has contrasted this type of terror with "agitational terror." The latter is used by those out of power, has different targets, and is employed for different reasons. See "Terror As a Weapon of Political Agitation," in Harry Eckstein, ed., *Internal War* (Glencoe, Illinois: Free Press, 1964), p. 72.

base area contributes to both of these objectives. If an insurgent movement can expand its base area, or base areas, it acquires a larger area from which to draw resources (manpower, intelligence, supplies).[17] If an insurgency expands its base area, it also by definition reduces the area over which the counterinsurgent has effective control. The resources available from that area become available to the insurgent instead of to the counterinsurgent.

The insurgent can improve the capabilities picture not only by *expanding* his base area but by *improving his control* of the area already held. It is obvious that insurgent influence in an area from which the movement hopes to draw resources may vary from almost zero to virtually total control. By and large, the greater the control over an area, the greater the percentage of that area's resources that the insurgents can hope to utilize.

Expansion of the base area provides an example of an objective that simultaneously satisfies military, economic, and political needs. Militarily the base area will provide a training ground, a staging area, a rest area, and a source of manpower. Economically it can be organized so its resources funnel into the insurgent movement and support it. Facilities for making small arms can be built there, and the base area can also provide food for the insurgents. Politically, it offers a basis for attempts to erode popular support for the incumbent regime. The *de facto* government established by the insurgents in the area also provides a basis for seeking foreign recognition of the insurgent movement.

Ideally a base area should be relatively inaccessible and should be a center of insurgent strength. A determined enemy will normally be capable of dislodging the rebels from their base area but, for reasons of cost, may not choose to do so. If the counterinsurgent should move against the base area, the insurgent will be tempted to contest control with him because of the importance of the area to the movement. The insurgent

17. For an excellent discussion of the importance of the base area, see Heilbrunn, *Partisan Warfare*, pp. 40–52. Heilbrunn, using a different analytic framework from the one employed here, considers expansion of the base area the most vital objective of insurgent strategy in a protracted war.

leadership must be careful at this juncture however not to jeopardize the movement's survival for the sake of a piece of land.[18]

Resource Reallocation

An insurgent movement is often dependent upon its enemy for logistical support. This is likely to be the case particularly at the outset of a conflict before the insurgents have been able to secure aid from abroad or set up their own armories in liberated areas. The insurgent may be able to divert enemy supplies to his own use by means of theft or graft. Thievery only works on an *ad hoc* basis and is apt to be risky. Collusion, on the other hand, based on bribery or on blackmail, can provide a safe and reliable access to supplies.[19]

Seizure by ambush remains the most popular way for insurgents to acquire counterinsurgent arms, ammunition, and supplies, however. At the same time that it provides needed material, an ambush also inflicts casualties, may demoralize enemy troops, may impress the populace, and may force the counterinsurgent to divert manpower from combat duty to the protection of convoys and fixed installations.

The typical ambush will involve a temporary roadblock, rapid annihilation of as many of the enemy as possible, speedy collection of enemy arms and ammunition, and a rapid withdrawal before the enemy can rally or can be reinforced. If intelligence can be counted on, the ambush is ideally suited to insurgent warfare. If the insurgent suffers from lack of radio equipment, this will force him to rely upon prearranged behavior, oral commands, and visual signs, and this may make it difficult for insurgent commanders to make rapid adjustments once the action has begun. A variation of the ambush is the double ambush perfected by the Viet Cong. A unit or convoy is ambushed, and the relief column hurrying to its aid is ambushed as well. Sometimes the Viet Cong attacked an isolated outpost or unit doing only enough damage to the

---

18. Ferdinand Otto Miksche describes such "redoubts" in Yugoslavia and Russia during World War II in *Secret Forces: The Technique of Underground Movements* (London: Faber, 1950), pp. 151–53.
19. It has been alleged that American supplies to Vietnam were sometimes diverted to the Viet Cong. See William J. Lederer, "Our Own Worst Enemy," *The Saturday Evening Post* (June 1, 1968), pp. 32–45.

"bait" to guarantee a call for help, their real interest being the ambush of the relief force.

The insurgent may wish to deny resources to the counterinsurgent by destroying them. The targets for destructive actions would include power plants, power lines, industrial installations, bridges, roads, tunnels, railroad tracks, railroad switching yards, trucks, railroad cars and engines, and communications facilities. Ambush is an appropriate technique for dealing with some of these and sabotage with others.[20]

If a country is industrialized and relatively small, and is therefore inhospitable to a rural-based insurgency, the insurgents may place heavy reliance upon sabotage. The impact of this activity upon the enemy can be substantial. In World War II the Danes engaged in 8500 separate sabotage operations against the German-controlled railroads. During World War I the railroad from Turkey to Medina, and its spurs into Palestine, was the focus of almost continual sabotage by T. E. Lawrence's Arab irregulars. Many locomotives were destroyed, engine drivers were led to strike, railroad travel was made nearly impossible, and Turkish troops were drawn into protecting the railroad.

Care must be taken in selecting sabotage targets lest local residents be made hostile toward the insurgents. Local residents are apt to have mixed feelings about violence that endangers their lives or their livelihoods, even if it also strikes at a hated invader. Guevara approached the problem in the following way.

. . . well-managed sabotage is always a very effective arm, though it should not be employed to put means of production out of action, leaving a sector of the population paralyzed (and thus without work) unless this paralysis affects the normal life of the society. It is ridiculous to carry out sabotage against a soft-drink factory, but it is absolutely correct and advisable to carry out sabotage against a power plant. In the first case, a certain number of workers are put out of a job but nothing is done to modify the rhythm of industrial life; in the second case, there will again be displaced workers, but this is entirely justified by the paralysis of the life of the region.[21]

20. See Heilbrunn, *Partisan Warfare*, for a detailed discussion of ambush and sabotage.
21. Guevara, *Guerrilla Warfare*, p. 16.

Demoralizing Enemy Forces

One way that the insurgent can seek to neutralize the manpower imbalance from which he suffers is to demoralize enemy troops and thus lower their effectiveness. The means at his disposal range from the most subtle psychological techniques to the use of techniques of terror. If there are a large number of acts of isolated harassment, such as sniping and the murder of individual enemy soldiers, enemy troops will become apprehensive. Ambushes will also contribute to demoralization. Repeated operations, such as those conducted by Vietminh Regiment Ninety-Five along the "street without joy,"[22] may make enemy troops skittish about even passing through the danger zone.

At the nonviolent end of the spectrum lie the techniques of propaganda. In his book, *Viet Cong*, Douglas Pike describes the *binh van* program in some detail.[23] According to Pike the following were the objectives of the *binh van* program, arranged in descending order of importance: (1) unit desertions to the NLF, preferably with an accompanying act of destruction; (2) individual desertion to the NLF; (3) individual or group defection without shifting allegiance; (4) provoking significant opposition within the military arm; (5) acts developing friction between Vietnamese officers and U. S. advisers; (6) covert pro-NLF activity in the enemy services; and (7) any act that might lower the morale of counterinsurgent personnel.[24]

The NLF placed special emphasis on use of family to demoralize a soldier. Letters from relatives, sometimes coupled with the application of selective terror against family members, was designed to lower the morale of the individual enemy soldier. Other techniques available to the insurgent include propaganda exploitation of deserters and prisoners, infiltration, mass demonstrations, rewards for desertion, terror against key leaders and elite units, and promises of liberal treatment for defectors.[25]

---

22. Operations along this stretch of roadway in Annam are described by Bernard B. Fall in Chapter 7 of *Street Without Joy* (Harrisburg, Penn.: The Stackpole Co., 1963).
23. Pike, *Viet Cong*, Chapter 14.
24. Ibid., pp. 256–58.
25. Ibid., pp. 259–68.

An innovation of the Chinese Communists, also used by the Cuban rebels, was that of offering prisoners a choice between serving with the insurgents, settling in insurgent territory, or returning to the former counterinsurgent unit. Galula considers a lenient policy toward prisoners the most effective way to demoralize enemy forces.[26] Castro's lieutenants would deliver a parting address to released prisoners in which the rebels' capacity to capture them again and again was stressed; an American reporter observed, "This expression of utter contempt for the fighting potential of the defeated had an almost physical impact on them. Some actually flinched as they listened."[27]

Inducing a Static Defense Posture
The insurgent is usually vulnerable to an aggressive and persistent mobile offensive on the part of the counterinsurgent. That being the case, it is in the interest of the insurgent to induce the counterinsurgent not to engage in that kind of offensive. The best way for the insurgent to do this is to conduct military operations that create pressing alternative demands for the use of counterinsurgent troops. If the insurgent can behave aggressively and conduct a large number of small but worrisome operations in widely separated parts of the country, he may create a serious dilemma for the counterinsurgent.

One response on the part of the counterinsurgent would be to withdraw his forces to the more secure, heavily populated areas. If the incumbent regime should choose to pull back to strong points, it will abandon the rural population and the resources of rural areas to the insurgent—a very dangerous long-term strategy.

A second response available to the incumbent regime would be to scatter its forces about the land in an effort to protect villages, towns, military installations, communications centers, and transportation hubs. If the insurgent can force this static

26. David Galula bases this conclusion on personal observation in the Chinese Civil War. Galula, *Counterinsurgency Warfare: Theory and Practice* (New York: Praeger, 1964), pp. 51–52.
27. Dickey Chapelle, "How Castro Won," in T. N. Greene, ed., *The Guerrilla—And How to Fight Him: Selections from the "Marine Corps Gazette"* (New York: Praeger, 1962), p. 223.

defensive posture upon the counterinsurgent, he will have achieved two important objectives. First, if enemy forces are busy defending various installations, they will not be available for mobile counterstrikes at insurgent units and vital base areas. Second, this defensive posture will leave the initiative to the insurgent. He can choose when and where to strike, for there are always more attractive targets than can be adequately defended. Isolated outposts can be overrun, truck convoys ambushed, power stations or power lines blown up, small units of enemy soldiers attacked, industrial installations attacked and destroyed. The counterinsurgent will lose men and supplies piecemeal to the insurgents, will begin to have morale problems, and will be frustrated by his inability to deal with the insurgent menace effectively.

If the insurgent, by the tempo and vigor of his actions, can dictate the strategy the counterinsurgent will use, he will have achieved a signal victory and may even have ensured the ultimate success of the insurgency. Neither of the two counterinsurgent strategies referred to above offers an efficient way of dealing with an insurgent threat. An incumbent regime might be able to crush an insurgent movement if it used one of these strategies, but its victory will be achieved despite its strategy (and because of disparity of resources), not because of it.

If the counterinsurgent should develop a third type of strategy, a combined strategy involving military strikes at the insurgents and a population utilization program, the challenge to the insurgent would be greater. The response alternatives of the counterinsurgent will be examined in the following chapter.

Increasing the Military Costs to the Counterinsurgent
There are a variety of ways in which the insurgent can increase the military cost of the conflict to the insurgents. A number of the techniques that can be employed, such as ambushes and raids, have already been discussed and need not be taken up again. The immediate objective may be to harass an enemy unit, to demoralize it, to defeat it, or to annihilate it. Beyond that, however, the insurgent objective may be to force the counterinsurgent to disperse his forces and, perhaps, to discourage him concerning ultimate victory.

Wherever the insurgent sees a cost to the counterinsurgent, he may try to increase it.

THE TACTICAL MIX AND THE EVOLUTION OF INSURGENCIES

The tactical principles of insurgent warfare differ from those of conventional warfare in part because of the extreme asymmetry of the capabilities of the two belligerents. Relative to the counterinsurgent, the insurgent is apt to lack manpower, firepower, airpower, transport, communications, military installations, logistic support, and territory.

The insurgent must seek ways to maximize his advantages while minimizing those of his opponent. This need thrusts him in the direction of a mobile warfare that relies upon good intelligence, surprise, avoidance, and speedy disengagement. Typically the insurgent will strike quickly, without warning, and often at night. He will try to make certain that conditions are heavily in his favor, and he will withdraw before the superior firepower of the enemy can be brought into play. When he withdraws he will seek to vanish into the countryside. His strikes are likely to be dotted over a large area to keep the counterinsurgent off balance.[28] Some of his operations may be directed toward enemy stores of arms and ammunition to overcome his own deficiency in this respect. His operations will normally involve small units. The Soviet partisan unit, the detachment, numbered 120 to 150 men. In Algeria, the ALN attempted to create battalions of up to 600 men, but they lacked mobility and were too easily detected by the French. In the winter of 1957 battalion size was reduced to 380. If the insurgent leadership is competent, operations will be characterized by careful prior planning. Regis Debray

---

28. He may seek to conduct operations in such a way as to conserve ammunition. Guevara cites one battle in which a machine gunner had to fire a rapid succession of bursts to slow the advance of Batista's forces. The gunner's Cuban compatriots assumed that his position had fallen since the principle of "saving fire" was being transgressed. *Guerrilla Warfare*, p. 14.

Observation of this principle may not have been as strict as Guevara would have us believe, however. Dickey Chapelle, in "How Castro Won," reports that the Fidelistas made "every mistake in the book—but one. They consistently delivered a high volume of fire. . . . They barely aimed and they did not conserve ammunition. But they consistently communicated their will to fight to an enemy whose superior equipment was unmatched by the will to use it."

has commented on Fidel Castro's planning. "The meticulous and almost obsessive attention Fidel paid to the smallest concrete detail of preparation for the most minor action, until the last day of the war, was amazing . . . the placing of fighters in an ambush operation; the number of bullets issued to each one; the path to be taken; the preparation and testing of mines; the inspection of provisions, etc. An excellent lesson in efficiency."[29] The planning of the insurgent leaders includes the detailed planning of specific operations, but it is not confined to that. As this study has emphasized, the insurgent leader must be concerned with a broad range of political, social, economic, and military questions. If he is to be effective, he must think in terms of resources, capabilities, an input mix, the behavior of the enemy, strategic objectives, and various tactical mixes.

Students of insurgency have shown a persistent interest in fashioning theories of insurgent evolution. The most popular of these is Mao Tse-tung's conception of a three-stage evolution of insurgent movements. In an early chapter it was made clear that this model is too rigid to be very helpful. Others have tried to specify the conditions for insurgent success. Otto Heilbrunn, for example, cities three fundamental requirements for success in a "revolutionary guerrilla war." "The first . . . was the availability of a detachment strong enough to annihilate or decisively defeat the enemy. The second was the defeat of the enemy. When local victory was achieved, the population, with guerrilla help, was roused to mass (anti-Japanese) struggles. This was the third condition for the establishment of a base: the awakening of the masses."[30]

A cursory examination of recent insurgencies, however, will show that these are not universal preconditions for success. The Algerian, Cypriot, Palestinian, and Tunisian insurgents did not achieve any of these fundamental requirements, much less all three of them. It is easy to mistake the familiar, or the desirable, for the universal. The notion of an "awakening of the masses" has romantic appeal and would doubtless be of value to an insurgency, but it is not indispensable.

29. Regis Debray, *Revolution in the Revolution*, trans. Bobbye Ortiz (New York: Grove Press, 1967), pp. 60–61.
30. Ibid., p. 41.

There is greater variety in insurgencies than is often acknowledged, and no single pattern of tactical evolution can do justice to all insurgencies. If one were to enumerate the specific tactics that insurgent movements might use and then note which of these tactics were used in conjunction with one another, one would find that insurgencies have utilized a variety of tactical mixes. Furthermore, one would discover that a given insurgency uses different tactical mixes at different stages of its development.

Nevertheless, for purposes of illustration, and being fully aware that no single pattern fits all insurgencies, it will be useful to suggest what a typical pattern of tactical evolution might look like. In table 1, the tactics and activities of a hypothetical insurgent movement are examined at five different points in time.

Table 1. Evolution of Insurgent Tactics

Specific Tactics	T_1	T_2	T_3	T_4	T_5
Recruitment of the discontented	x	x	x	x	x
Development of political apparatus	x	x	x	x	x
Distribution of subversive literature		x	x	x	
Coalition formation		x	x	x	
Demonstrations		x	x	x	
Strikes		x	x	x	
Formation of mass organizations		x	x	x	x
Threats			x	x	
Seizure of hostages			x	x	
Theft, graft, and blackmail			x	x	
Ambushes			x	x	
Attacks on isolated outposts			x	x	
Selective terror (agitational)			x	x	
Isolated harassment of CI forces			x	x	
Formation of *de facto* government			x		
Announcement of insurgent program			x		
Release or conversion of prisoners			x	x	
Sabotage			x	x	x
Propaganda campaign vs. CI forces			x	x	x
Public "trials" of enemies				x	x
Expansion of base areas				x	x
Selective terror (enforcement)				x	x
Some large-scale military operations				x	
Political delegations set abroad				x	x
Conventional warfare					x

At Time 1, the movement is just beginning to take shape. Leaders are beginning to recruit followers and to develop a political apparatus. As the movement grows, it begins to engage in a wider range of political activities and to undertake some military operations (T_3). In a later stage of development, the movement begins to shoulder the burden of extensive administrative responsibilities in liberated areas. Parallel to its guerrilla activities it also begins to undertake some conventional military operations (T_4). When the insurgents become strong enough to engage counterinsurgent troops on a large scale, the agitational type of political activity that characterized the earlier stages of the conflict is likely to become less prominent (T_5). At this point, the insurgency has been transformed into essentially a civil war (or, in the case of insurgency against a colonial power or an invading army, a quasi-conventional war against a foreign power).

CHAPTER VII
THE COUNTERINSURGENT

THE CONTEXT OF COUNTERINSURGENCY

▬▬▬ The discussion in this chapter will parallel that of the preceding two chapters. It will examine the context of counterinsurgency and will discuss some of the strategies, tactics, and special problems that counterinsurgent leaders must consider.

In conventional warfare, the principles of strategy and tactics apply equally well to both antagonists. In insurgent warfare, on the other hand, the course of action that the insurgent tries to pursue with regard to the counterinsurgent is quite different from that which the counterinsurgent tries to pursue with regard to the insurgent. The difference in strategy and tactics is grounded in the disparity between the resources of the counterinsurgent and those of the insurgent. The counterinsurgent will typically have a distinct advantage in such things as manpower, firepower, airpower, transport, communications, and apparatus for population utilization. Because the strategic and tactical principles of insurgent warfare are different from those of conventional warfare, each side has much to learn. One must learn to fight a stronger foe; the other must learn to fight a foe who is weaker and who therefore wants to change the rules of the game. Each must learn to conduct a struggle that is both military and political, a struggle in which the contours of public attitudes and behavior may be as important as terrain contours and in which major victories may be won without either side firing a shot.

There is little room for tactical and strategic dogmatism in insurgent warfare, and the advantage lies with the side that learns quickly and adapts more easily. For the counterinsurgent there is no one "best" strategy or tactic. There is not even any one mix of strategies and tactics that is invariably best. Which mix is best depends upon the total situation, including the resources and behavior of the insurgent, the resources and strategic situation of the counterinsurgent, and the general situation with regard to the populace. For example, the strategic hamlet plan, which held the key to victory in Malaya, proved ineffective in Vietnam.

SITUATIONAL FACTORS

The Physical and Demographic Environment

The physical and demographic features of a country are not as critical for the counterinsurgent as they are to the insurgent, but they do have an impact upon counterinsurgent strategy and tactics. Because he is weaker, the insurgent must try to conduct his activities in areas and under conditions that neutralize the counterinsurgent's generally superior strength and technology. Even under conditions in which he can use surprise, speed, and elusiveness his advantage may be slight and temporary. The counterinsurgent, because he is stronger, can operate under a wider variety of environmental conditions. Terrain, vegetation, and climate may create problems for him and neutralize some of his capabilities, but only rarely will survival be dependent upon them. For example, the use of aircraft in Kenya allowed the British to spot and attack Mau Mau detachments from the air. The survival of the Mau Mau was at stake but not the survival of the British units.

One reason the physical and demographic features of a country are important to the counterinsurgent is because this will determine the number, size, and location of the areas favorable to guerrilla operations. If the areas favorable to insurgent operations are few, small, and isolated, counterinsurgent forces may try to eliminate the insurgents in a given area by sealing off the area and starving the insurgents into submission. The process would be repeated in one area after another. On the other hand, if terrain and other conditions allowed it, the security forces might enter an area and attempt to hunt down the insurgents. An example of this type of effort was seen in Bolivia in 1968 when army units, aided by Indians, hunted down and eliminated the entire insurgent force. It was in a climactic engagement during this campaign that Che Guevara lost his life.

If the areas favorable to insurgent operations are numerous and difficult to isolate, a different approach may be employed.

Some military units might be used to harass the insurgents in these areas while other units might be employed in security and population control activities. At the same time, political and economic reforms might be introduced to blunt insurgent appeal to the populace. This pattern would be similar to the one used successfully in Malaya.

Physical and demographic features may influence counterinsurgent strategy, but they are not the only influences on strategy, and they may not even be the most important influences. If the counterinsurgent possesses an advanced technology, terrain features may be less important than would otherwise be the case. For example, aircraft may increase his reconnaissance, attack, and airlift capabilities and reduce the significance of mountainous areas. Radar and other electronic devices can markedly improve his surveillance ability. It is hard to imagine a modern T. E. Lawrence operating in the desert against an enemy equipped with modern aircraft. To be sure, the counterinsurgent may become overly dependent on his advanced equipment and may not be able to liberate himself from it. Apparently the French in Indo China became excessively dependent on mobile armored units and oriented most of their thinking toward operations with such units. As the French became road-bound, the Viet Minh forces were able to move through the countryside and to control it. They could strike against units moving along the roads or against isolated strongholds and then fall back, knowing the French had little taste for nonmechanized pursuit.

The Insurgent

A factor that shapes the environment in which the counterinsurgent operates is, of course, the insurgency itself. The record indicates that one of the most difficult tasks which an incumbent regime faces is to recognize that an insurgency exists and that it is a real threat. Until the counterinsurgent regime recognizes that its existence is being threatened, it is likely to find it difficult to develop the sense of urgency that is required if the challenge is to be met effectively. The activities of a new insurgency are likely to be on a small scale, and the incumbent regime may be inclined to treat these activities as isolated phenomena which can be ignored or dealt with by normal police activity. The government may fear that it will lose face if it acknowledges that its citizens have taken arms against it or that it will simply call attention to the movement and encourage it by organizing to control it.

When the counterinsurgent leadership recognizes that the movement must be taken seriously, its initial reaction is likely to be to make a military response. This response will probably take the form of an attempt to use the armed forces in a conventional way. The army is equipped for conventional combat, and officers and men have been trained for it and only for it. A substantial reorientation is usually necessary before an army can respond effectively to an insurgent challenge. Officers must learn to ask new questions: Who is our enemy? What are his objectives? What strategy is he utilizing? What tactical mix is he utilizing? What are his vulnerabilities and how may we best strike against him? This reorientation is difficult and time consuming at best; at worst, it may prove impossible. The slowness of the counterinsurgent in recognizing the challenge and in adjusting to it may be one of the greatest advantages that the insurgent possesses.

A second element in a counterinsurgent response may be a heavy emphasis upon repression. A government that finds it difficult to strike directly at the guerrilla may attempt to strike at him indirectly by utilizing control measures and a counterterror. This may, of course, be counterproductive. When Batista's regime in Cuba relied on repression and terror, it antagonized many who had previously been indifferent to it, and it drove a number of young men into the hills for refuge. Some of these young men subsequently fought for Castro.

Counterinsurgent regimes have found it difficult to understand that the insurgent challenge is a politico-military one and that it requires a political response as well as a military response. They tend to conceive of the problem as essentially one of maintaining law and order and are slow to consider the introduction of basic social, political, and economic reforms.

Traditions and Expectations
Sometimes incumbent regimes do seek to introduce reforms. The government of Magsaysay in the Philippines introduced land reform and other reforms. In Bolivia land reform was

also introduced. This path is often a difficult one, however. The government may well be caught in a squeeze between the demands of citizens for a greater share in the resources of the country and the competing demands of powerful groups in the country whose support the government needs if it is to stay in power. Various technical problems may also impede land reform. In the central highlands of South Vietnam, for example, competitive claims to land ownership were advanced by Vietnamese, Montagnards, Chinese, and French.

In the case of invasion and a resulting insurgency, a somewhat similar situation may exist with regard to land reform. The invasion may have made substantial demands on the resources of the invader, and combatting the insurgency places further demands on his resources. The immediate interest of the invader, therefore, may lie not in instituting reforms desired by the populace but in finding ways to draw the maximum amount of resources out of the country. Japanese policy in China from 1940 to 1945 illustrates this point.[1] Initial attempts at economic reform soon gave way to harsh punitive measures.

The resources available to a government are apt to be great compared with those available to the insurgent, yet a government almost always feels that its resources are inadequate and are stretched to the breaking point. It feels that it is the focal point for competing demands that cannot all be satisfied. Furthermore, as is obvious, the government must also carry on the normal functions of government. That confers certain advantages, but it also carries disadvantages with it in the form of demands on its limited supply of skills, energies, and resources. If the government does not continue to perform such governmental functions as protection of the populace, it will lose support. The insurgents charge that the government is incompetent to do its job properly and then seek to demonstrate the truth of their charge by making the government's job impossible.

One of the situational factors that serves as a constraint on the counterinsurgent is the image that the regime has within

1. See Chalmers A. Johnson, *Peasant Nationalism and Communist Power: The Emergence of Revolutionary China, 1939–1945* (Stanford, Calif.: Stanford University Press, 1962).

the country. The insurgent movement can create an image and a reputation that it hopes will contribute to the achievement of its goals. The incumbent regime is not in a position to radically alter its image, however. It must live with the image that it has earned. This may be a negative factor (the French in Indo China, the Batista government in Cuba) or a positive factor (the British in Malaya). Whether negative or positive, the image and reputation of the counterinsurgent will have a great impact upon the ability of the incumbent regime to utilize the population and resources of the country. For example, a government such as Batista's, which had the reputation of being autocratic, harsh, and unresponsive, could not gain much from the institution of limited social or economic reforms. The government that waits for an insurgency to develop before taking an interest in reform may have waited too long. The options open to it may have contracted, and the actions that might once have been sufficient to forestall trouble may now appear inadequate and insincere.

The International Environment
Insurgent movements are often highly dependent upon outside support. An appropriate counterinsurgent strategy, therefore, is that of trying to cut off the insurgent from the international environment and to thwart his efforts to get support from it. Sometimes, however, the counterinsurgent may not give sufficient weight to this consideration. During the rise of the Castro movement in Cuba, a series of articles on Castro and his movement appeared in United States newspapers such as the *New York Times*. This publicity played an important part in shaping the way the international environment came to view the Batista regime and its insurgent opponents. In this case, it was Batista who was isolated and cut off from outside support.

To accomplish his aim of isolating the insurgent, the counterinsurgent may rely upon diplomacy, propaganda, control of communications and travel, and military operations. Since the insurgency must normally have some reasonable prospect of victory before it can gain support from abroad, the counterinsurgent will seek to demonstrate that the movement is small and weak with no prospect of victory. It will also seek to present the insurgency in an unfavorable light, perhaps as a group of self-seeking bandits or fugitives from justice.

In addition to trying to prevent the insurgent from gaining assistance from the international environment the incumbent regime may seek help for itself. If the counterinsurgent receives foreign support, he may encounter the same problem faced by the insurgent—that of maintaining autonomy. Conflicts in Southeast Asia have demonstrated how domestic insurgencies can become internationalized. In such cases one or both parties may lose freedom of action.

CAPABILITIES AND BASIC INPUTS

Leadership is a vitally important input factor in any insurgency, and the names of charismatic insurgent leaders come to mind easily—Mao Tse-tung, Castro, Guevara, Ho Chi Minh, Tito, T. E. Lawrence. This does not mean that leadership is less important to the counterinsurgent than to the insurgent. It may suggest, however, that insurgency, because it is dramatic, tends to attract the dramatic personality.

The kind of leadership called for by insurgency is different from that demanded by counterinsurgency. The same array of qualities appears to be needed, but the various qualities are needed in different proportions. It is vitally important that the insurgent leader be able to raise the spirits of his men and generate faith and confidence when the situation looks dark. The counterinsurgent leader, on the other hand, functions as the head of a government and can manage with little in the way of charisma. It is important that the insurgent leader have administrative abilities, for he must create an organization and see to its operation. For the counterinsurgent leader, however, this quality is absolutely essential. He must oversee the functioning of an army, supervise a large nonmilitary administrative apparatus, supervise the development and utilization of the resources of a nation, and adjust the competing demands of groups within the country. Magsaysay was greatly aided in his campaign against the Huks by his ability to develop a series of programs utilizing a wide range of governmental capabilities.

The administrative machine that the counterinsurgent leader inherits is usually one that was formed by evolution and circumstance. It is likely to be cumbersome and inefficient yet very hard to change. Key positions may be held by unqualified appointees who are more interested in prestige and personal gain than in accomplishing assigned tasks. His personnel needs may exceed the number of skilled and dedicated technicians and civil servants available. The counterinsurgent leader, if he understands his problems, may lament that his responsibilities exceed the capabilities of the organization that he commands.

A political capacity must go hand in hand with managerial capabilities. Governments in countries in which insurgencies are occurring are often unstable, and the head of the government must build and maintain political support as a prerequisite to undertaking social, political, or economic reforms or a vigorous counterinsurgent program. In most cases, while reforms may benefit some, they will hurt others. The reforms that the counterinsurgent leader may wish to insitute are likely to be costly to his supporters. His problem, therefore, assuming that he wishes to institute reforms, is how to do it without eroding the basis of his own support. In short, while the resources that are at the disposal of the government may be great in theory, in fact those resources may only be available if the leader is determined and politically skilled.

Effective population utilization is important to both the insurgent and the counterinsurgent. Each side must utilize the population effectively if essential needs are to be met. The insurgent, for example, needs to draw recruits from the population. The counterinsurgent also needs manpower for its forces and must seek to cut off the flow of manpower to the insurgents. The counterinsurgent has a recruiting advantage denied to the insurgent, for the government can introduce conscription. In liberated areas that it controls, the insurgent can do virtually the same, of course.

The government has a marked advantage when it comes to the logistic input. The government may feel that its resources are inadequate to meet the demands made upon them, but its plight will almost never be as serious as that of the insurgent. The government can tax, appropriate, borrow, and it can receive aid from abroad. Furthermore, it has less of a problem transporting material. It can use trucks, trains, planes, and carts openly and subject only to the danger of ambush. If it receives military aid from abroad, ocean-going ships can tie up in its harbors and unload hundreds of tons of equipment. The insurgent leadership, on the other hand, may have to devote an inordinate amount of time arranging the smuggling of small quantities of arms into the country. The insurgent must worry about acquiring resources, and the counterinsurgent must worry about managing the resources he has. Management not only includes getting resources of the right kind to the right place at the right time, it also means denying those resources to the enemy. This is no small task. The counterinsurgent sometimes supplies both himself and his opponent.

COUNTERINSURGENT STRATEGY AND TACTICS

The main objective of counterinsurgent leaders will usually be the retention of political power. What they will do with their power if they stay in office is another question. They may want to maintain the social, political, and economic *status quo,* or they may want to preside over a program of gradual and moderate change.

They would like to retain power at the least possible cost, but if it is necessary they will be prepared to pay a very high cost. Their interest in holding down the cost of retaining power does not reflect an abstract concern for cost efficiency but their concern with staying in office. The more costly the struggle against the insurgency, the greater are the resource demands that the counterinsurgent leader must make on elements within the society that have supported him.

When designing a program to counter the insurgent movement, the counterinsurgent leadership should focus on the basic input factors of the insurgents (i.e., leadership, organization, population utilization, manpower, intelligence, and logistics). It should see if there are ways of reducing the supply of each input to the insurgents or increasing its cost. If the supply of a given input is already a problem for the insurgent, the counterinsurgent should do what it can to further aggravate the problem.

Magsaysay's anti-Huk campaign in the Philippines is illustrative. To undermine insurgent leadership and create uncertainty within the movement, he established a system of financial rewards for information leading to the capture of key insurgent leaders. To reduce popular support for the insurgency, he encouraged his soldiers to make friends with the people wherever possible, ordering them to repair roads and bridges, build schoolhouses, provide medicines and medical help, and mix with the people on a friendly basis. To reduce the manpower input, he offered amnesty to the insurgents and gave land and homes to those who defected and were willing to be relocated. To reduce the flow of intelligence to the insurgents, he made it clear that severe action would be taken against those who informed against the government. To reduce the flow of weapons to the insurgents, he established a monetary reward for serviceable unlicensed weapons which were turned in.

If the insurgency is deriving significant support outside the country, the counterinsurgent may try to interfere with this support. These efforts may take the form of improved border patrols so material cannot reach the insurgent and so the insurgent cannot make use of privileged sanctuary in a neighboring country. They may take the form of diplomatic actions aimed at denying the insurgent material and funds from a neighboring country or training and sanctuary in that country.

To decide which strategy or tactic to employ, the counterinsurgent must take several things into account: (1) whether he possesses the capabilities needed to employ the strategy or tactic; (2) whether its use fits into his over-all political, military, and psychological objectives; and (3) what benefits are to be realized from its use in relation to the cost of its use. It is often easy to tell if the first condition is met but more difficult to tell if the second condition is satisfied. The use of a particular strategy or tactic might not fit the over-all objectives of the counterinsurgent. The destruction of a village, for example, might wipe out a few insurgents but be counterproductive psychologically and politically.

The third question is often still harder to answer with confidence. Any course of action that the counterinsurgent considers will have certain benefits and costs associated with it. Costs include any and all disadvantages that will result from the use of the strategy or tactic under consideration. They may be economic, political, psychological, or military and are likely to be difficult to estimate with any precision. In addition, for planning purposes, the counterinsurgent will want to be able to compare the costs and benefits of competing strategic and tactical proposals.

The remainder of the chapter will examine some of the courses of action open to the counterinsurgent. The figure below suggests the relationship to one another of goals, objectives, targets and tactics.

Goal	Objectives	Targets	Tactics
		Population	Destroy Ins. Pol. Org. Psych. Opns. Public Relations Military Civic Action Pop. & Res. Control Pol. & Econ. Reforms
Retain Power	Alter Capabilities (i.e., Increase those of counter-insurgent and decrease those of insurgent)	Insurgent Organization	Defeat Ins. Forces Undermine Ins. Morale Deny Base Areas Deny Resources Amnesty Programs Intel./Counterintel.
		International Audience	Sympathetic World Opin. Diplomatic Support Material Support Military Support

Fig. 1.

Psychological Activities

The counterinsurgent may undertake psychological operations aimed at the population in general and at particular targets such as the armed services and those who support the insurgents. The objective of a given operation will vary depending upon the specific target but will probably fall into one or the other of the following broad categories: continuation of favorable behavior; adoption of favorable behavior; temporary deterrence of unfavorable behavior; discontinuance of unfavorable behavior. The various techniques that are used contribute, in one way or another, to the processes of coercion, persuasion, and conditioning.

The counterinsurgent will have control of such media as exist in the country and will be able to mobilize them to some extent in support of his efforts. The availability of the media, however, may lead him to rely upon them unduly. In developing nations the effectiveness of the mass media is limited, and governmental concentration upon them may involve neglect of face-to-face communication. The insurgent, in turn, may place heavy reliance upon face-to-face communication since the media are not available to him. This has been the pattern in Vietnam. Sometimes, of course, the counterinsurgent may make intensive use of face-to-face contact as the French did for a time in Algeria.[2]

The incumbent regime will normally try to picture the insurgency in an unfavorable light. It may try to portray the insurgent leaders as bandits, as terrorists, or as dupes of a foreign power. If this effort is successful the insurgents may find themselves isolated from the people, and they may also find that the recruitment rate is dropping and the desertion rate climbing.

If the counterinsurgent can weaken or remove the insurgent's will to fight, his task will be much eased. In designing a program to achieve this end, an amnesty program can play an important part. When the insurgent movement is enjoying success, few insurgents may take advantage of the opportunity to return peacefully to their homes. On the other hand, when the weather is bad, when the insurgents are being harried by counterinsurgent troops, when the movement has suffered defeats, and when victory seems almost hopeless, the opportunity to return to the comforts of home and family may begin to appear attractive. If, at that time, the incumbent regime can take actions to show that it means to right political and social wrongs, it may be able to defeat the insurgent movement from below. The individual insurgent, making his

2. Edgar O'Ballance, *The Algerian Insurrection, 1954–62* (Hamden, Conn.: Archon Books, 1967), pp. 95–96.

own personal calculation of costs and benefits, may conclude that the benefits of continued participation are outweighed by the risks and discomforts. The killing of insurgents is not the only way to defeat an insurgent movement.

Civic Action
After an incumbent regime has been struggling against an insurgent movement for a time it usually becomes clear to that regime that its relations with the populace are a matter of critical importance. In any campaign by the government to broaden its base of popular support, the army is likely to play a prominent role. The behavior of the army can have a great influence on the way that the incumbent regime will be perceived by the people. This is understandable since the army is a symbol of government that the people often contact. A government's effort to improve its relations with the people can be easily undermined if the army behaves in a harsh and arrogant way.

If the army and its resources are used properly, it can be an important factor in improving relations between government and people. Its officers and men can show compassion for the people while engaging in combat near villages and can be careful and helpful. In addition, when not engaged in combat activities, troops can be used on projects needed by local communities—building schools, giving medical care, teaching children and adults to read, improving the water supply. In some cases the net benefits from the civic action programs of the army may be greater than from its counterguerrilla activities. One of the decisions that the counterinsurgent leadership must make concerns the proportion in which the army's energies will be devoted to civic action programs and counterguerrilla activities. Valuable as civic action programs are, however, the people also look to the military to provide security. The diversion of troops to civic action projects when insurgent military activity constituted a serious threat to the people might well be counterproductive. Civic action programs can best be employed in areas where enemy activity is low.

Population and Resource Control Programs
A population and resources control program seeks to deny to the insurgent the human and material resources needed to

continue the insurgency. The design features of such a program will depend upon the sources of guerrilla support. If the insurgent is receiving substantial support from external sources, one of the aims of the program will be to seal the border and prohibit movement of goods or personnel from the border to internal areas. If the main sources of supply are indigenous, the program will aim at controlling the movement of persons and resources within the country.

The counterinsurgency effort in Malaya offers an example of a successful population and resources control program. Family pictures were taken, and families were spot checked from time to time. All members of a family had to be accounted for. Identification cards were issued and checked frequently. In some villages central eating facilities were established and identification cards were required for entrance to meals. Production and distribution of food was carefully controlled to prevent it from falling into the hands of the insurgents. Curfews were established. Travel was curtailed and carefully controlled. Strangers in a village were easily noticed and observed. The strategic hamlet program was used in conjunction with clear-and-hold operations in the hope that the two together would gradually destroy the insurgent command system. "This has two simultaneous effects; first, it forces the insurgent units to fight to support their infrastructure at the point at which government forces are at their most concentrated and strongest, thereby automatically increasing the contact-and-kill ratio; and, second, it reduces their sources of supplies and new recruits. The reason for the success which will be gained from this type of operation is that the government forces are fighting in the *same element* and for the same purpose (control of the population) as the insurgent forces."[3]

The administration of a population and resources control program of this kind is very burdensome, and its cost is very great. Furthermore, it is likely to be extremely inconvenient for the people and force a remodeling of their lives. The counterinsurgent will need to consider carefully whether the potential gains from such a program will outweigh potential

3. Sir Robert Thompson, *Defeating Communist Insurgency: The Lessons of Malaya and Vietnam* (New York: Praeger, 1966), pp. 116–17.

costs. If such a program is to be instituted, it must be embarked upon in a whole-hearted way. A half-hearted program might be sufficient to antagonize the populace without being energetic enough to interdict the flow of resources to the insurgent. In such a situation, the program would be clearly counterproductive. The loss of popular support might well be accompanied by an increased flow of intelligence and recruits to the insurgent movement.

Since these programs, when successful, eliminate the village as a base for guerrilla support, insurgents are strongly opposed to them.[4] In Vietnam the insurgents tried to discredit the resettlement centers as concentration camps and argued that they were meant to deny land ownership to the small farmer. "The strategic hamlet was portrayed as a technique for depriving farmers of land (the land on which the village was built) or as a means of swindling farmers out of good land in exchange for bad. Cadres asserted that the GVN represented the rich landlords and pursued a false land reform scheme; that GVN land taxes were unreasonable; that the 'U.S.-Diem clique' confiscated millions of hectares of the best rice land for military purposes such as building military bases."[5]

MILITARY AND RELATED ACTIVITIES

An insurgency is a politico-military phenomenon. If the counterinsurgent centers his attention exclusively on the military aspects or the political aspects of the problem he is likely to be defeated. To be effective, the counterinsurgent must wage political and military campaigns simultaneously. These campaigns must be closely co-ordinated. If the boundaries of military districts are drawn on the basis of terrain and do not take political realities into consideration, the opportunity for unco-ordinated action will be great. In Vietnam, for example, the military undertook a "search and clear" operation in an area just before harvest time. To protect the people while the area was being cleared, they were relocated in refugee centers in another area. By the time the military operation was com-

---

4. Douglas Pike, *Viet Cong* (Cambridge, Mass.: M.I.T. Press, 1966), p. 116.
5. Ibid., p. 276.

pleted, the crops had rotted in the field and the efforts at political consolidation in the area had been nullified.[6]

The counterinsurgent must establish his political and military goals, but he must understand that the strategy and tactics appropriate to one area may be inappropriate in another. In one part of a country, companies and battalions may engage in tactics that are very nearly conventional. In another section small units may be relied upon. These units may operate over wide areas, concentrating on raids, ambushes, reconnaissance, and political action.

The counterinsurgent, with limited forces, must try to defend vital installations, protect the population, protect his lines of communications, and carry the fight to the insurgent in the latter's sanctuary areas. He must determine how each of these tasks is to be performed and what proportion of available energies and resources should be devoted to each to maximize results. He must decide which insurgent initiatives to respond to and what actions to initiate to carry the fight to the insurgent. Because of his fixed obligations, it is not usually possible for the counterinsurgent to seize and maintain the military initiative unless his troops outnumber those of the insurgent in a ratio of fifteen to one or more. Much depends, of course, on the quality and training of the troops, available firepower, the quality of the intelligence being used, and the mobility of the troops. For both military and psychological reasons it is important that the government forces be able to react quickly when the insurgent strikes. This quick reaction capability may be achieved by the use of motor vehicles, helicopters, or rapid movement on foot across country. To be effective, mobility must also be combined with an efficient high-speed communications system.

The counterinsurgent leadership will be interested in attacking the insurgent control system and in defending its own control system. Sometimes force will be used for these purposes. The counterinsurgent control system is visible to the insurgent and relatively easy to strike at, but the reverse is not equally true. The insurgent's control system operates underground. Its leaders are wanted men. Outlawing the insurgent

6. William Corson, *The Betrayal* (New York: W. W. Norton & Co., 1968), pp. 67-71.

organization may discourage young men from joining it and make it harder for the organization to function, but it will rarely destroy it.

The most effective weapon to use against the insurgent control network is intelligence. Intelligence may come from defectors, prisoners of war, agents working within guerrilla units, and sympathetic members of the population. The last mentioned source is dependent upon the establishment of a communications system which will transmit information efficiently without revealing its source and making individuals vulnerable to reprisal. An example of such an arrangement is the census grievance system in South Vietnam. A trusted member of the community is hired by the government to listen to the grievances of the local inhabitants. Individuals talk to this official privately, and it is hard for insurgent observers to know which individuals are providing intelligence and which are not.

The insurgent movement may attempt to use violence and intimidation against the counterinsurgent control system, as in Vietnam. The counterinsurgent apparatus must try to defend itself physically against these attacks if possible, and it may also try to use political techniques in its defense. It may try to overcome corruption in its ranks or simply silence those who suggest that there is corruption. It may try to improve the economic situation or silence critics of that situation. It may follow the path of reform in the hope of psychologically isolating insurgent terrorists, or it may institute elaborate control measures in an effort to apprehend them.

BIBLIOGRAPHY AND INDEX

SELECTED BIBLIOGRAPHY

American Society for Political and Legal Philosophy. *Revolution: Nomos VIII*. Edited by Carl J. Friedrich. New York: Atherton Press, 1966.
Black, Cyril E., and Thornton, Thomas P., eds. *Communism and Revolution*. Princeton: Princeton University Press, 1964.
Brinton, Crane. *The Anatomy of Revolution*. Rev. ed. New York: Prentice-Hall, 1952.
Campbell, Arthur. *Guerrillas: A History and Analysis*. New York: The John May Company, 1968.
Chorley, Katherine C. *Armies and the Art of Revolution*. London: Faber and Faber Ltd., 1943.
Clissold, Stephen. *Whirlwind: An Account of Marshal Tito's Rise to Power*. London: The Cresset Press, 1949.
Condit, D. M. *Case Study in Guerrilla War: Greece During World War II*. Washington: Special Operations Research Office, 1961.
——. *Challenge and Response in Internal Conflict*. 3 vols. Washington: Center for Research in Social Systems, 1967.
Coser, Lewis A. *Continuities in the Study of Social Conflict*. New York: Free Press, 1967.
——. *The Functions of Social Conflict*. New York: The Free Press of Glencoe, 1956.
Cross, James Eliot. *Conflict in the Shadows: The Nature and Politics of Guerrilla War*. New York: Doubleday, 1963.
Crozier, Brian. *The Rebels: A Study of Post-War Insurrections*. Boston: Beacon Press, 1960.
Davies, James C. "Political Stability and Instability: Some Manifestations and Causes." *Journal of Conflict Resolution* 13 (March 1969): 1–18.
——. "Toward a Theory of Revolution." *American Sociological Review* 27 (1962): 5–19.
Debray, Regis. *Revolution in the Revolution?* Translated by Bobbye Ortiz. New York: Grove Press, 1967.
Deitchman, Seymour J. *Limited War and American Defense Policy*. Cambridge, Mass.: M.I.T. Press, 1964.
Denton, Frank H., and Phillips, Warren. "Some Patterns in the History of Violence." *Journal of Conflict Resolution* 12 (March 1968): 182–95.
Dinerstein, Herbert S. *Intervention Against Communism*. Baltimore: Johns Hopkins Press, 1967.

Eckstein, Harry, ed. *Internal War*. New York: Macmillan, 1964.
Fall, Bernard B. *Last Reflections on a War*. New York: Doubleday, 1967.
———. *Street Without Joy*. Harrisburg, Penn.: The Stackpole Co., 1963.
———. *The Two Viet-Nams: A Political and Military Analysis*. 2d ed., rev. New York: Praeger, 1967.
———. *Viet-Nam Witness 1953–66*. New York: Praeger, 1966.
Feierabend, Ivo K., and Feierabend, Rosaline L. "Aggressive Behaviors Within Polities, 1948–1962: A Cross-National Study." *Journal of Conflict Resolution* 10 (1966): 249–71.
Galula, David. *Counterinsurgency Warfare: Theory and Practice*. New York: Praeger, 1964.
Giap, Vo-nguyen. *People's War, People's Army: The Viet Cong Insurrection Manual for Underdeveloped Countries*. New York: Praeger, 1962.
Greene, T. N., ed. *The Guerrilla—And How to Fight Him: Selections from the "Marine Corps Gazette."* New York: Praeger, 1962.
Guevara, Ernesto (Che). *Guerrilla Warfare*. New York: Random House, 1968.
Gurr, Ted. "A Causal Model of Civil Strife: A Comparative Analysis Using New Indices." *American Political Science Review* 62 (December 1968): 1104–25.
———. "Psychological Factors in Civil Violence." *World Politics* 20 (January 1968): 245–78.
Halperin, Morton H. *Limited War in the Nuclear Age*. New York: John Wiley and Sons, 1963.
Heilbrunn, Otto. *Partisan Warfare*. New York: Praeger, 1962.
———. *Warfare in the Enemy's Rear*. New York: Praeger, 1963.
Huntington, Samuel P. "Political Development and Political Decay." *World Politics* 17 (April 1965): 386–430.
———. *Political Order in Changing Societies*. New Haven: Yale University Press, 1968.
Johnson, Chalmers A. *Peasant Nationalism and Communist Power: The Emergence of Revolutionary China, 1939–1945*. Stanford, Calif.: Stanford University Press, 1962.
———. *Revolution and the Social System*. Hoover Institution Studies, no. 2. Stanford: Hoover Institution, 1964.
———. *Revolutionary Change*. Boston: Little, Brown and Co., 1966.
Jureidini, Paul A.; LaCharite, Norman A.; Cooper, Bert H.; and Lybrand, William A. *Casebook on Insurgency and Revolutionary Warfare: XXIII Summary Accounts*. Washington: American University Special Operations Research Office, 1962.
Lasswell, Harold D., and Lerner, Daniel. *World Revolutionary Elites*. Cambridge, Mass.: M.I.T. Press, 1968.

SELECTED BIBLIOGRAPHY • 135

Lawrence, T. E. *Seven Pillars of Wisdom.* New York: Doubleday, 1935.
Leiden, Carl, and Schmitt, Karl M. *The Politics of Violence: Revolution in the Modern World.* Englewood Cliffs: Prentice-Hall, 1968.
Lieuwen, Edwin. *Arms and Politics in Latin America.* New York: Published for the Council on Foreign Relations by Praeger, 1960.
McColl, Robert W. "A Political Geography of Revolution: China, Vietnam, and Thailand." *Journal of Conflict Resolution* 11 (1967): 153–67.
McCuen, John J. *The Art of Counter-Revolutionary War: The Strategy of Counter-insurgency.* Harrisburg, Pa.: Stackpole Books, 1966.
Mao Tse-Tung. *Selected Military Writings.* Peking: Foreign Language Press, 1963.
Martz, John D. *Central America: The Crisis and the Challenge.* Chapel Hill: U.N.C. Press, 1959.
Miksche, Ferdinand Otto. *Secret Forces: The Technique of Underground Movements.* London: Faber, 1950.
Mitchell, Edward J. "Inequality and Insurgency: A Statistical Study of South Vietnam." *World Politics* 20 (April 1968): 421–38.
―――. "Some Econometrics of the Huk Rebellion." *American Political Science Review* 67 (December 1969): 1159–72.
Modelski, George. *The International Relations of Internal War.* Research Monograph no. 11. Center of International Studies. Princeton, N.J.: Princeton University Press, 1961.
Molnar, Andrew R. *Undergrounds in Insurgent, Revolutionary, and Resistance Warfare.* Washington: Special Operations Research Office, 1963.
Nasution, Abdul Haris. *Fundamentals of Guerrilla Warfare.* New York: Praeger, 1965.
Ney, Virgil. *Notes on Guerrilla War: Principles and Practices.* Washington: Command Publication, 1961.
O'Ballance, Edgar. *The Algerian Insurrection, 1954–62.* Hamden, Conn.: Archon Books, 1967.
―――. *The Greek Civil War, 1944–1949.* New York: Praeger, 1966.
―――. *The Indo-China War, 1945–1954: A Study in Guerrilla Warfare.* London: Faber and Faber, 1964.
―――. *Malaya: The Communist Insurgent War, 1948–1960.* London: Faber and Faber, 1966.
Osanka, Franklin M., ed. *Modern Guerrilla Warfare—Fighting Communist Guerrilla Movements, 1941–1961.* New York: The Free Press of Glencoe, 1962.
Paget, Julian. *Counter-Insurgency Operations: Techniques of*

Guerrilla Warfare. New York: Walker and Company, 1967.
Paret, Peter. *French Revolutionary Warfare from Indochina to Algeria: The Analysis of a Political and Military Doctrine.* New York: Praeger, 1964.
———, and Shy, John W. *Guerrillas in the 1960's.* Rev. ed. New York: Praeger, 1966.
Pike, Douglas. *Viet Cong.* Cambridge, Mass.: M.I.T. Press, 1966.
Pustay, John S. *Counterinsurgency Warfare.* New York: Free Press, 1965.
Pye, Lucian W. *Guerrilla Communism in Malaya, Its Social and Political Meaning.* Princeton: Princeton University Press, 1956.
Rigg, Robert B. *How to Stay Alive in Vietnam.* Harrisburg, Pa.: Stackpole, 1966.
Rosenau, James N., ed. *International Aspects of Civil Strife.* Princeton: Princeton University Press, 1964.
Rummel, R. J. "Dimensions of Conflict Behavior Within and Between Nations, 1958–60." *Journal of Conflict Resolution* 10 (1966): 65–73.
Sanger, Richard H. *Insurgent Era: New Patterns of Political, Economic and Social Revolution.* Washington: Potomac Books, 1966.
Stanger, Roland J., ed. *Essays on Intervention.* Columbus: Ohio State University Press, 1964.
Stone, Lawrence. "Theories of Revolution." *World Politics* 18 (1966): 159–77.
Taber, Robert. *The War of the Flea: A Study of Guerrilla Warfare Theory and Practice.* New York: Lyle Stuart, Inc., 1965.
Tankam, George K. *Communist Revolutionary Warfare: From the Vietminh to the Vietcong.* Rev. ed. New York: Praeger, 1967.
Tanter, Raymond. "Dimensions of Conflict Behavior Within and Between Nations, 1958–60." *Journal of Conflict Resolution* 10 (1966): 48–64.
———, and Midlarsky, Manus. "A Theory of Revolution." *Journal of Conflict Resolution* 11 (1967): 264–80.
Thayer, Charles W. *Guerrilla.* New York: Harper and Row, 1963.
Thompson, Sir Robert. *Defeating Communist Insurgency: The Lessons of Malaya and Vietnam.* New York: Praeger, 1966.
Valeriano, Napoleon D., and Bohannan, Charles T. R. *Counter-Guerrilla Operations: The Philippine Experience.* New York: Praeger, 1962.
Wolf, Charles, Jr. *United States Policy and the Third World: Problems and Analysis.* Boston: Little, Brown and Co., 1967.
Zawodny, J. K., ed. "Unconventional Warfare." *The Annals of the American Academy of Political and Social Science* 341 (May 1962): 1–107.

INDEX

A
Algeria, 4, 25, 32, 33, 58–59, 72–75, 77, 86–88, 98–99, 109–10, 124
Americans, in Philippines, 22, in Vietnam, 72, 73, 75, 106, 127
Angola, 99n
Arabs, 3, 61, 78, 105

B
Bargaining, 83–87
Batista, Fulgencio, 97, 116, 118
Bolivia, 114, 116
British, in Norway, 22; in Malaya, 35, 114, 118
Broz, Josip ("Tito"), 3, 20, 51, 77, 97

C
Castro, Fidel, vi, 4, 51, 61, 98, 107, 110, 116, 118
Chapelle, Dickey, 107n, 109n
Chetnik movement, 20
Chiang Kai Shek, 3
China, 3, 8, 117
Chinese Communists, 8, 76, 95, 107
Chinese Nationalists, 101
Climate, 73–74
Cold War, 4
Communist, insurgency in Greece, 61, 91; thinking on revolution, 95n
Corson, William, 128n
Counterinsurgency, 74–75, 113–29; and insurgency, model, 28–50; strategy and tactics, 33–35, 41, 121–29; psychological factors, 33–35, 41, 123; leadership, 119–20; population utilization, 120–21, 125–27; intelligence, 129
Cuba, vi, 4, 61, 77, 89, 107, 116–18
Cyprus, vi, 73, 86, 88, 96, 110

D
Debray, Régis, 109, 110n
Declaration of Independence, 23
Deitchman, Seymour, 79n
Deutsch, Karl, 78n
Diem, 76, 100, 127

E
Eckstein, Harry, 5n, 102n
Economic analysis, vi, 41, 51–71
Economic exploitation, 17, 21
EOKA (National Organization of Cypriot Combatants). *See* Cyprus
Escalation, 9, 44–50, 83

F
Fall, Bernard B., 91n, 106n
Feierabend, Ivor, 16n
Feierabend, Rosalind, 16n
FLN. *See* Algeria
French, resistance, World War II, 3, 20, 26; in Indo China, 9, 25, 59, 115, 117–18; in Algeria, 72, 74–75, 87, 98–99, 109, 124

G
Galula, David, 73–74, 107
Germany, resistance to, 3, 20, 22, 25–26, 33, 42, 77, 97, 105
Giap, Vo Nguyen, 9, 91
Greece, 4, 61, 77, 91
Guerrilla, 3, 90, 92
Guevara, Ernesto "Che," 51, 114; thought, 45, 73, 89, 90, 105, 109n
Gurr, Ted, 16n
GVN (Government of Vietnam), 127

H
Halperin, Morton, 79n
Heilbrunn, Otto, 97n, 103n, 105n, 110
Ho Chi Minh, 4, 51
Ho Chi Minh Trail, 73
Huks, 4, 32, 119, 121

I

Ideology, 7, 52, 54
Indo China, 4, 25, 59, 74, 115
Input-output analysis, 21–24, 51–71
Insurgency, analysis of, v, vi, 89; stages in, v, vi, 7–10; defined, 5; psychological aspects of, 5, 7, 10, 11; relationship to irregular warfare, 10; typology of, 14–27; genesis of, 16–20; and counter-insurgency, model, 28–50; context of, 72–88
Insurgent movements, leadership, 11, 21, 51–52; intelligence, 11, 24, 56–58; organization, 11, 21, 52–53; communication, 11; recruitment and training, 11, 12, 53–55; equipment and logistics, 11, 22, 57; discipline and morale, 12, 55; strategy and tactics, 13, 24–25, 35, 89–112; objectives, 20–21, 81–87 *passim*, 92–93; population utilization and manpower, 23, 53–54, 58–65, 95–102
Intelligence, 11, 24, 56–58, 129
Internal war, 14
International environment, 26, 77–79, 93, 118
Internationalization, 26, 78, 119
Intervention, 4, 5, 7, 26
Irregular warfare, relationship to insurgency, 10

J

Japan, war against, 76, 101, 110, 117
Johnson, Chalmers A., 76n, 77, 117

K

Kenya, 114

L

Land reform, 116–17
Latin America, 97
Lawrence, Thomas Edward, 3, 51, 61, 99, 105, 115
Lederer, William L., 104n
Leiden, Carl, 98n
Limited warfare, 4, 79–83

M

McNamara, Robert, v
Magsaysay, Ramón R., 116, 119, 121
Malaya, 4, 35, 59, 77, 98, 114–15, 126
Mao Tse-Tung, 3, 8, 51, 101; thought, v, 91, 95, 110
Maquis, 3
Mau Mau, 114
Midlarsky, Manus, 14n, 16n
Mikhailovitch, Draza, 3, 97
Miksche, Ferdinand Otto, 104n
Military. *See* Insurgency, Counter-insurgency
MNA (Algerian National Movement), 59
Modelski, George, 78n, 79
MRLA (Malayan Races Liberation Army). *See* Malaya
Murray, J. C., Colonel, 91

N

Nationalism, 24
Negotiation, 83–87
NLF (National Liberation Front), of Vietnam, 77, 98, 100–101, 104, 106; of Algeria. *See* Algeria

O

O' Ballance, Edgar, 124n

P

Palestine, 88, 105, 110
Paret, Peter, 95n
Partisans, 15, 26, 77, 109
Philippines, 4, 22, 32, 77, 116, 119, 121
Pike, Douglas, 79, 100–101, 106, 127
Police, 96, 102, 116
Population utilization, insurgent, 23, 58–65, 95–102; counterinsurgent, 96, 120, 125–27
Psychological warfare, 7, 33, 76
Pye, Lucian W., 5n, 98n

R

Resistance, to Germany in World War II, 15, 26, 33; Yugoslav, 3, 25, 26, 42, 77, 97; Russian, 3,

22; French, 3, 20, 26; Dutch, 26, 53
Rosenau, James N., 78n
Rummel, R. J., 14n
Russia. See Soviet Union

S
Schelling, Thomas C., 82, 85n
Schmitt, Karl M., 98n
Self-determination, 17, 21
Shy, John W., 95n
Soviet Union, 3, 22, 53, 104, 109,
Stalin, Joseph, 53, 77
Strategy. See Insurgency, Counterinsurgency
Substitutability, 66-71
Systems analysis, vi, 28-50

T
Tanter, Raymond, 14n, 16n
Terror, 60, 63, 97-99, 102
Thomson, Sir Robert, 98n, 100n, 126n
Thornton, Thomas P., 102n
"Tito." See Broz, Josip

Tunisia, 88, 110
Turkey, 3, 105

U
United States, 127; advisers, 106. See also Americans

V
Viet Cong. See NLF
Vietminh, 9, 25, 59, 74, 77, 106, 115
Vietnam, 4, 6, 32-33, 60, 72-76 passim, 98, 100-101, 106, 114, 117, 124, 127, 129. See also Indo China

W
Warsaw, 73
Wolf, Charles, 60n

Y
Yugoslavia, 20, 25, 26, 42, 77, 97, 104

Z
Zawodny, J. K., 77

www.ingramcontent.com/pod-product-compliance
Lightning Source LLC
Chambersburg PA
CBHW030115010526
44116CB00005B/258